Page 23

S0-AFN-391

TASTE
OF THE
TOWN

A Collection of Recipes from

Talk
OF THE
TOWN
and
NewsChannel 5

No claim is made as to the originality of these recipes.
Each has been tested and adapted by the individual
who submitted it.

Published by Landmark Television of Tennessee, Inc.
NewsChannel 5 - **Talk of the Town**

Copyright Landmark Television of Tennessee, Inc.
474 James Robertson Parkway
Nashville, Tennessee 37219

All photos from NewsChannel 5 Archives
Special thanks to Lucy Ray

Edited, Designed and Manufactured by
FRP™
2451 Atrium Way   Nashville, Tennessee 37214

Book Design by Mark Föltz

Manufactured in the United States of America

First Printing, 1996   12,500 copies
Library of Congress Number: 96-079255
ISBN: 0-9654961-0-4
Copyright 1996

Table of Contents

Foreword...6

NewsChannel 5 Facts..7

...and they can cook, too! Recipes from NewsChannel 5 9

Beverages and Appetizers 27

Soups and Salads...39

Vegetables and Sides...69

Main Dishes...85

Breads...139

Desserts 155

Index...186

Order Form...191

Foreword

Talk of the Town hosts
Meryll Rose, Joe Case and Harry Chapman

If you've ever watched **Talk of the Town**, you know we love to cook,
and we love to eat! And our viewers do too! The recipes have always been
one of the most popular features of our show, and people have often asked
us why there's not a **Talk of the Town** cookbook.
Well, after 12 years, we're proud to say, here it is!

We've included the most-requested recipes from your favorite chefs,
as well as some personal recipes from our NewsChannel 5 family. You'll
also enjoy some vintage pictures as we look back at some of the
milestones in the history of NewsChannel 5.

We hope you enjoy the cookbook, and most of all, we thank you for inviting
us into your home each day. Whether we're cooking or learning something
new or just sharing a laugh, it's better because we share it with you!

Thanks for watching **Talk of the Town**, and happy cooking!

–Talk of the Town
November, 1996

NewsChannel 5
Facts

▲ ▲ ▲

In 1974 NewsChannel 5 was the first Nashville station with a female co-anchor. Oprah Winfrey got her start at NewsChannel 5 long before becoming popular as a talk show host.

▲ ▲ ▲

In 1996, NewsChannel 5 became the first Nashville television station to program a second channel out of one building (NewsChannel 5+).

▲ ▲ ▲

The broadcast in 1986 of The 28th Annual Grammy Awards on NewsChannel 5 was the first stereo broadcast of any Nashville television station.

▲ ▲ ▲

NewsChannel 5 began reporting school closings in the late 1960s. Snow Watch continues to be very popular today, with more up-to-date reports than ever before.

▲ ▲ ▲

NewsChannel 5 signed on the air in 1954 with the first full-height tower in Tennessee.

▲ ▲ ▲

NewsChannel**5**
Facts

▲ ▲ ▲

In 1964, NewsChannel 5
was the first Nashville station to provide
statewide election coverage.
Here, Dan Rather and Chris Clark anchor
election coverage in 1970.

▲ ▲ ▲

*NewsChannel 5 was the first Nashville
station with ENG
(Electronic News Gathering)-1974.*

▲ ▲ ▲

*NewsChannel 5 was the first
Tennessee television station with a
female Vice-President (Ruth Talley, 1966).*

▲ ▲ ▲

*NewsChannel 5 was the first Nashville station
to operate a satellite truck (1985).*

▲ ▲ ▲

The popular **Hee Haw** *was originally produced
at NewsChannel 5
and featured popular entertainers
like Roy Rogers.*

▲ ▲ ▲

Chapter 1

...and they can cook, too!

Recipes from NewsChannel 5

NewsChannel 5 has always had a commitment
to raising money for organizations in need. This "Polio
Fund" broadcast with Minnie Pearl aired in 1956.

NewsChannel 5

*The NewsChannel 5 Female Anchors:
Lydia Lenker, Vicki Yates,
and Amy Marsalis.*

*The NewsChannel 5 Sports Team:
Hope Hines and Mark Howard.*

Stuffed Grape Leaves (Dolmades)

Nick Beres, NewsChannel 5 Reporter and Cook

1 pound ground beef
1 egg, beaten
1 medium onion, chopped
½ cup uncooked rice
½ cup chopped parsley
2 cloves garlic, chopped
2 tablespoons pine nuts
2 tablespoons olive oil
  Salt and pepper to taste
¼ cup water
1 jar grape leaves
1½ cups beef broth

▲ Mix the ground beef and the egg in a large bowl. Add the onion, rice, parsley, garlic, pine nuts, olive oil, salt, pepper and water, stirring well.

▲ Soak the grape leaves in hot water for 5 minutes; drain. Separate the leaves. Place one leaf on a plate coated with olive oil. Place a spoonful of the ground beef mixture on the leaf. Roll up to enclose the filling, tucking in the ends. Repeat with the remaining leaves.

▲ Place the stuffed grape leaves seam side down in a large saucepan. Add the beef broth and enough water to completely cover the stuffed leaves. Place a heatproof plate on top to keep the leaves in place.

▲ Cook, covered, over medium heat for 45 minutes. Cool and serve with lemon.

Serves 12 to 15

An old Greek recipe he learned from his grandma.

Pasta-Vegetable Soup

Lydia Lenker, NewsChannel 5 Anchor

4   cups canned salt-free undiluted chicken broth
3   cups water
1   cup sun-dried tomatoes (without salt or oil)
6   ounces bowtie pasta, uncooked
4   green onions, sliced
1   tablespoon balsamic vinegar
1   clove garlic, minced
1   (10-ounce) package frozen spinach, thawed, drained

▲ Combine the chicken broth, water and sun-dried tomatoes in a large saucepan. Bring to a boil; reduce heat. Simmer, covered, for 10 minutes or until the tomatoes are softened.

▲ Remove the tomatoes with a slotted spoon; cool. Cut into thin strips. Return to the saucepan. Add the pasta, green onions, vinegar and garlic.

▲ Bring to a boil; reduce heat. Simmer, covered, for 15 minutes or until the pasta is tender. Remove from the heat. Stir in the spinach.

▲ Serve with crusty French bread.

Serves 9

Christmas Chili

Lydia Lenker, NewsChannel 5 Anchor

2   pounds lean ground beef
1   large green bell pepper, chopped
1   large onion, chopped
1   large clove garlic, minced
1⅓ cups chili powder
1   (28-ounce) can tomatoes
1   (6-ounce) can tomato paste
¾   cup water
1½ teaspoons salt
1   teaspoon sugar
⅛   teaspoon crushed red peppers (optional)
2   (16-ounce) cans red kidney beans or pinto beans

▲ Brown the ground beef, green pepper, onion and garlic in a large saucepan, stirring until the ground beef is crumbly; drain.

▲ Stir in the chili powder. Add the tomatoes, tomato paste, water, salt, sugar and crushed red peppers. Bring to a boil over medium-high heat.

▲ Cook for 40 minutes, stirring occasionally. Add the beans.

▲ Simmer for 15 minutes longer, stirring occasionally.

▲ May substitute 2 chopped green chiles for the crushed red peppers.

Serves 6 to 8

...and they can cook too!

Vegetarian Chili

Beth Tucker, NewsChannel 5 Anchor

1 large onion, chopped
2 cloves garlic, minced
2 tablespoons canola oil
1 envelope chili mix
2 (16-ounce) cans chopped tomatoes with green chiles
1 cup textured vegetable protein granules (TVP)
2 (16-ounce) cans chili-hot kidney beans
1 (28-ounce) can whole tomatoes
  Hot sauce, salt and pepper to taste

▲ Sauté the onion and garlic in the oil in a large saucepan until tender. Add the chili mix and chopped tomatoes with green chiles.

▲ Bring to a low boil. Stir in the protein granules.

▲ Simmer for 5 to 10 minutes, stirring occasionally. Add the beans and whole tomatoes. Break up the tomatoes with a spoon or spatula.

▲ Cook, covered, over low heat for 30 minutes, stirring occasionally. Season with hot sauce, salt and pepper.

Serves 8

5 This recipe is for very hot chili. If you like it milder, then substitute another large can of tomatoes for the tomatoes with green chiles, and use regular kidney beans instead of the hot chili beans. For a soupier chili, add additional water or tomato juice. The textured vegetable protein granules—a dried soy product very high in protein and very low in fat—are available at health food stores. The granules soak up the cooking liquids and their flavors and have the consistency of ground beef. They are good to use instead of ground beef in spaghetti sauces, sloppy Joes and lasagna. Don't worry; this is not tofu!

Pan Salad

*Sharon Frost, **Talk of the Town** "Soap Maven"*

1   (3-ounce) package lime gelatin
1   (3-ounce) package lemon gelatin
1   cup hot water
1½ cups cold water
1   (12-ounce) can crushed pineapple
3   bananas, chopped
½   package miniature marshmallows
½   cup sugar
1   tablespoon cornstarch
1   egg, beaten
½   cup whipping cream
    Sugar to taste
    Juice of ½ lemon
½   teaspoon vanilla extract
1   cup shredded sharp Cheddar
    cheese

▲ Dissolve the lime and lemon gelatin in the hot water in a bowl. Stir in the cold water.

▲ Drain the pineapple, reserving 1 cup of the juice. Add the pineapple, bananas and marshmallows to the gelatin mixture, stirring well.

▲ Pour into a 9x13-inch dish. Chill until firm.

▲ Combine the sugar, cornstarch, egg and the reserved pineapple juice in a saucepan.

▲ Bring to a boil. Cook until the mixture thickens, stirring constantly. Chill thoroughly.

▲ Beat the whipping cream in a mixer bowl until soft peaks form. Add the sugar, lemon juice and vanilla, beating until stiff peaks form. Fold into the chilled pineapple juice mixture.

▲ Spread over the congealed gelatin mixture. Top with the cheese.

Serves 10 to 12

5 This recipe is one that has been served at my family's Christmas dinners and other special occasions for generations. I must give credit to my Aunt Puddin' for sharing this family secret with me. She's as sweet as this recipe. I have often used this for bridal luncheons and teas. It makes a great dish with homemade chicken salad sandwiches or just as dessert.

...and they can cook too!

Asparagus Casserole

Ron Howes, NewChannel 5 Meteorologist, and wife Cyndy Howes

1   (4-ounce) jar sliced mushrooms
1   cup herb-seasoned stuffing or croutons
½   cup melted margarine or butter
1   (16-ounce) can asparagus spears, drained
½   cup chopped onion
¼   cup flour
½   teaspoon white pepper
½   teaspoon dry mustard
1   cup half-and-half
¼   cup grated Parmesan cheese

▲ Drain the mushrooms, reserving the liquid. Combine the stuffing, ¼ cup of the margarine and the reserved mushroom liquid in a bowl and mix well. Spread in a shallow baking dish.

▲ Arrange the asparagus spears over the prepared layer. Sauté the mushrooms and onion in the remaining ¼ cup margarine in a saucepan until tender. Stir in the flour, white pepper and dry mustard.

▲ Add the half-and-half gradually, mixing well after each addition. Cook over medium heat until thickened, stirring constantly. Pour over the asparagus; sprinkle with the cheese.

▲ Bake at 375 degrees for 20 minutes. May layer sliced hard-cooked eggs over the asparagus for a meatless luncheon dish.

Serves 6

Sweet Potato Casserole

Amy Marsalis, NewsChannel 5 Anchor

This is my mom's recipe. We enjoy this dish at Thanksgiving dinners—it's what I think of as comfort food!

3   cups mashed sweet potatoes
½   cup sugar
2   eggs, beaten
½   cup melted butter
1   teaspoon vanilla extract
⅓   cup milk
⅓   cup butter, softened
1   cup packed brown sugar
½   cup flour
1   cup chopped pecans

▲ Combine the sweet potatoes, sugar, eggs, melted butter, vanilla and milk in a large mixer bowl. Beat at medium speed until smooth.

▲ Spoon the mixture into a greased 2-quart baking dish.

▲ Mix the softened butter, brown sugar, flour and pecans in a small bowl until crumbly. Sprinkle over the sweet potatoes.

▲ Bake at 350 degrees for 25 minutes.

Serves 6 to 8

Eggs Fiesta

*Harry Chapman, **Talk of the Town** Host, and wife Angela Chapman*

1   pound bulk sausage
2   tablespoons butter, softened
6   slices bread
1   cup sliced mushrooms
1   green bell pepper, finely chopped
¼   cup chopped green onions
⅔   cup chopped tomatoes
6   ounces grated sharp Cheddar cheese
5   eggs
2   cups half-and-half
1   teaspoon salt
⅛   teaspoon pepper
½   teaspoon dry mustard

▲ Brown the sausage in a skillet, stirring until crumbly. Drain well and set aside.

▲ Spread butter on the bread slices and cut bread into 1-inch pieces. Arrange buttered side up over the bottom of a 9x13-inch baking dish.

▲ Layer with the sausage, mushrooms, green pepper, green onions, tomatoes and cheese.

▲ Beat the eggs, half-and-half, salt, pepper and mustard in a medium bowl. Pour over the layers. Chill, covered, for 6 hours to overnight.

▲ Bake, uncovered, at 350 degrees for 45 minutes.

Serves 6

TASTE OF **5** THE TOWN

...and they can cook too!

Hopping John *real good*

Chris Clark, NewsChannel 5 Anchor, and wife Gloria Clark

2	cups rice
2	slices bacon
1	(16-ounce) can black-eyed peas
1	medium onion, chopped
1	pound lean ground beef
	Salt and pepper to taste
⅛	teaspoon garlic powder
¼	teaspoon oregano
2	cups prepared creamy coleslaw
	Hot sauce to taste

▲ Cook the rice using package directions; set aside.

▲ Fry the bacon in a medium skillet until crispy. Remove and crumble the bacon, reserving the pan drippings.

▲ Combine the bacon and the black-eyed peas in a small saucepan. Simmer until heated through.

▲ Sauté the onion in the reserved pan drippings until translucent. Add the ground beef, salt, pepper, garlic powder and oregano. Cook until the ground beef is browned and crumbly, stirring frequently. Drain well.

▲ Layer the rice, black-eyed peas, coleslaw and ground beef mixture on serving plates. Serve the hot sauce on the side.

Serves 4 to 6

5 Back in 1963, Chris was doing a show in Albany, Georgia, and he announced to all of South Georgia that he really missed a dish he enjoyed at the University of Georgia called "Hopping John," and that his new bride had never even heard of it. He got lots of sympathy, and I got a lot of recipes—all very different. I chose this one because it was most like the one Chris remembered, and the lady who sent it said I'd have a happy husband if I served it often. It worked!

Sportsman's Casserole

Hope Hines, NewsChannel 5 Sports Director

2 pounds lean stew meat, cubed
2 (10-ounce) cans low-fat cream of mushroom soup
1 envelope onion soup mix
1 cup dry white wine
1 (6-ounce) can sliced mushrooms, drained
   Cooked rice

▲ Combine the stew meat, mushroom soup, onion soup mix, wine and mushrooms in a 3-quart baking dish, mixing well.

▲ Bake, tightly covered, at 350 degrees for 4 hours, stirring occasionally. The longer it is cooked, the better it is.

▲ Spoon over cooked rice to serve.

Serves 6

Mark's "Lasagna of Love"

Mark Howard, NewsChannel 5 Weekend Sports Anchor

1 pound ground beef
1 pound sausage
2 (20-ounce) jars spaghetti sauce
24 ounces mozzarella cheese, shredded
1 to 2 cups grated Parmesan cheese
9 lasagna noodles, uncooked

▲ Brown the ground beef and sausage in a large skillet, stirring until crumbly; drain. Add half of the spaghetti sauce.

▲ Simmer over medium heat until heated through, stirring occasionally.

▲ Spoon a small amount of the remaining spaghetti sauce in a 9x13-inch baking dish. Layer the noodles, meat sauce, remaining spaghetti sauce, mozzarella cheese and Parmesan cheese 1/3 at a time in prepared dish.

▲ Bake, covered with foil, at 350 degrees for 40 minutes; remove the foil. Bake for 5 minutes longer. Let stand for 10 minutes before serving.

Serves 6

 Mark says that everyone knows he's serious about a woman when he prepares this recipe for her.

Shrimp and Spanish Rice

Vicki Yates, NewsChannel 5 Anchor

1½ cups rice

2½ cups water

1 teaspoon salt

1 Vidalia onion, chopped

1 tablespoon butter or margarine

2 (6-ounce) cans tomato sauce

1 green bell pepper, chopped
   Pepper to taste

1 to 2 teaspoons Cavender's Cajun
   spices

1 pound shrimp

▲ Cook the rice in water with salt in a saucepan until all the liquid has been absorbed.

▲ Brown the onion in butter in a small skillet until translucent. Add to the rice.

▲ Stir in the tomato sauce, green pepper and pepper. Cover and keep warm.

▲ Bring a large saucepan of water to a boil. Add the Cajun spices and the shrimp.

▲ Cook until the shrimp turn pink; drain.

▲ Serve the shrimp on the side, or peel and add to the rice mixture. Add a salad and crusty French bread for a great meal.

Serves 4

 This is a recipe my children like a lot.

Shrimp Stroganoff

*Meryll Rose, **Talk of the Town** Host*

8   ounces medium egg noodles
1   cup sour cream
1   (10-ounce) can cream of mushroom soup
1   teaspoon dried whole dillweed
¼   cup sliced green onions
16 black olives, pitted, sliced
1   cup shredded Cheddar cheese
1   pound shrimp, cooked, peeled

▲ Cook the noodles using package directions. Drain and set aside.

▲ Combine the sour cream, mushroom soup and dillweed in a large bowl; mix well. Add the green onions, olives, ½ cup of the cheese and the shrimp, stirring well. Stir in the noodles gently. Spoon into a greased 2-quart baking dish.

▲ Bake, covered, at 350 degrees for 30 minutes. Uncover and sprinkle with the remaining ½ cup cheese.

▲ Bake for 5 minutes longer or until the cheese is melted.

Serves 6 to 8

5 This has been a favorite recipe for my family. A dear friend brought this to us the night we came home from the hospital after the birth of our daughter, Lauren, and it was such an elegant meal after eating bland hospital food! Now, it's always the first recipe I think of when I'm taking a meal to a friend!

Meryll's Garden Salsa

*Meryll Rose, **Talk of the Town** Host*

4   cups chopped tomatoes
2   cups chopped green bell peppers
1   cup each chopped hot peppers and chopped cilantro
2   cloves garlic, minced
2   (6-ounce) cans tomato paste
2   teaspoons lime juice
1½   teaspoons salt
2   tablespoons sugar
¼   teaspoon ground cumin
¾   cup cider vinegar

▲ Combine the tomatoes, green peppers, hot peppers, cilantro, garlic, tomato paste, lime juice, salt, sugar, cumin and vinegar in a large saucepan.

▲ Cook over medium-high heat until heated through but not boiling, stirring often. Pour into hot sterilized half-pint jars, leaving ¼-inch headspace; seal with 2-piece lids. Process in a hot water bath for 30 minutes. Refrigerate jars after opening.

▲ May omit the tomato paste for thinner salsa.

Makes 6 half-pints

Angel Hair Pomodoro

Sharon Frost, ***Talk of the Town*** *"Soap Maven"*

16 ounces angel hair pasta

1 small onion, chopped

3 tablespoons minced fresh garlic

½ cup minced fresh basil

1 tablespoon vegetable oil
Dash of wine (optional)

2 (16-ounce) cans chopped
tomatoes

8 ounces freshly grated Parmesan
cheese

3 tablespoons chopped green olives
(optional)

▲ Cook the pasta using package directions. Drain and set aside.

▲ Sauté the onion, garlic and basil in the oil in a large saucepan. Add wine if desired.

▲ Stir in the tomatoes. Bring the mixture to a boil. Add the cheese, stirring until the cheese begins to melt. Add the pasta a little at a time, stirring well to coat. Add the green olives.

▲ Spoon onto serving plates and garnish with a sprig of basil and more Parmesan cheese.

▲ May prepare Alfredo sauce by sautéing 1 tablespoon minced garlic in 2 tablespoons butter. Stir in 2 cups heavy cream, ½ teaspoon grated nutmeg and 8 ounces grated Parmesan cheese. Add half of the pasta to the sauce, stirring to coat. Serve half Angel Hair Pomodoro and half Angel Hair Alfredo.

5 This is a simplified version of a recipe that I learned from Kenny Rogers. Once, at his house, he had the chef from "Spago's" come to teach about 6 of us how to make this dish, which is one of Kenny's favorites. He often serves half a bowl of the Angel Hair Pomodoro and half a bowl of Angel Hair Alfredo. The chef taught us to heat, cool, peel, deseed and chop the fresh tomatoes like the French do, but when I'm in a hurry I just use canned tomatoes.

Apples with Cranberries

Martha Underwood, Office Manager, NewsChannel 5 Newsroom

2 cups fresh cranberries

3 cups quartered apples

1 cup sugar

1 tablespoon lemon juice

½ cup packed brown sugar

½ cup rolled oats

¼ cup flour

⅓ cup margarine, softened

▲ Combine the cranberries, apples, sugar and lemon juice in a 1½-quart baking dish.

▲ Mix the brown sugar, oats, flour and margarine in a small bowl, stirring until crumbly. Sprinkle over the fruit.

▲ Bake at 350 degrees for 1 hour or until bubbly.

Serves 6

Cheesecake

Martha Underwood, Office Manager, NewsChannel 5 Newsroom

½ cup raisins

8 ounces cream cheese, softened

2 tablespoons margarine, softened

½ cup sugar

1 egg

2 tablespoons flour

⅔ cup milk

¼ cup lemon juice

1 (9-inch) graham cracker pie shell

▲ Soak the raisins in hot water to cover in a bowl until softened; drain well.

▲ Beat the cream cheese, margarine, sugar and egg in a mixer bowl until light and fluffy. Add the flour, milk and lemon juice, beating well. Fold in the raisins.

▲ Spoon into the pie shell. Garnish with graham cracker crumbs.

▲ Bake at 350 degrees for 35 minutes. Cool slightly. Chill before serving.

Serves 6 to 8

5 This lady is sort of the Newsroom mother. She is known for her famous birthday cakes.

TASTE OF **5** THE TOWN

…and they can cook too!

Momma Case's Biscuit Puddin'

*Joe Case, NewsChannel 5 Weatherman and **Talk of the Town** Host, and wife Pam Case*

(Warning: Do not read further if you're watching cholesterol, fat or anything else unhealthy!!!)

3 eggs

4 cups milk

6 biscuits, crumbled

2 slices bread, cubed

2 cups sugar

1 teaspoon vanilla extract

¾ cup margarine, melted

▲ Beat the eggs and milk in a small bowl. Pour over the biscuits and bread in a large bowl. Stir in the sugar, vanilla and margarine. Spoon into a baking dish.

▲ Bake at 350 degrees for 45 minutes or until a knife inserted near the center comes out clean.

Serves 6

 Momma Case was my grandmother, whose sole responsibility was keeping the entire Case clan "fat 'n happy"!!

Fudge Pie

Martha Underwood, Office Manager, NewsChannel 5 Newsroom

¼ cup sifted flour

1 cup sugar

3 tablespoons baking cocoa

½ cup melted butter

2 eggs, beaten

½ cup chopped nuts

1 teaspoon vanilla extract

1 (8-inch) unbaked pie shell

▲ Sift the flour, sugar and baking cocoa together into a large bowl. Add the melted butter, mixing well. Stir in the eggs. Fold in the nuts and the vanilla. Pour into the pie shell.

▲ Bake at 350 degrees for 35 minutes. Cool before slicing.

Serves 6

Blueberry Peach Cake

Elizabeth Owen, NewsChannel 5 Consumer Specialist

1   cup sifted flour

1   teaspoon baking powder

½   cup butter, softened

½   cup packed light brown sugar

½   cup sugar

2   large eggs

2   cups peeled, thinly sliced ripe peaches

1   cup fresh blueberries

1   tablespoon fresh lemon juice

½   teaspoon ground cinnamon

3   tablespoons sugar

▲ Whisk the flour and baking powder together in a medium bowl.

▲ Cream the butter, brown sugar and sugar at high speed in a large mixer bowl for 3 minutes or until light and fluffy. Add the flour mixture, beating at medium speed just until blended.

▲ Add the eggs, beating until smooth. Spread the batter in a buttered and lightly floured 8-inch square baking pan. Layer with the peaches and blueberries. Drizzle with the lemon juice. Sprinkle with a mixture of the cinnamon and sugar.

▲ Bake at 350 degrees for 1 hour or until golden brown. Serve warm with ice cream or whipped cream.

Serves 6 to 8

Chocolate-Filled Snowballs

Elizabeth Owen, NewsChannel 5 Consumer Specialist

1   cup unsalted butter, softened

¾   cup sugar

1   tablespoon brandy

2   cups flour, sifted

1   cup chopped pecans

8   ounces Hershey's chocolate kisses

    Confectioners' sugar

▲ Cream the butter, sugar and brandy in a mixer bowl until light and fluffy. Add the flour and pecans, mixing well.

▲ Shape the dough into a ball; wrap in plastic wrap. Chill for at least 30 minutes.

▲ Remove the foil from the kisses. Cover each one with the dough, forming 1-inch balls. Place on an ungreased cookie sheet.

▲ Bake at 375 degrees for 12 minutes or until lightly browned.

▲ Sprinkle with confectioners' sugar while warm. Roll in the confectioners' sugar to coat when cooled. Store in an airtight container.

Makes 2 to 2½ dozen cookies

 This is my favorite Christmas cookie to give to friends.

My Boys' Favorite Lemon Cake

*Debbie Alan, former **Talk of the Town** Host*

1   (2-layer) package lemon cake mix
1   (3-ounce) package lemon gelatin
4   eggs, beaten
¾   cup water
¾   cup vegetable oil
½   cup lemon juice
2   cups confectioners' sugar

▲ Combine the cake mix, lemon gelatin, eggs, water and oil in a large bowl; beat well. Pour into a greased 9x13-inch cake pan.

▲ Bake at 350 degrees for 30 minutes. Remove from the oven and pierce several times with a fork.

▲ Beat the lemon juice and confectioners' sugar in a mixer bowl until smooth. Drizzle over the warm cake.

Serves 12 to 15

Aunt Lulu's White Butter Cake

*Harry Chapman, **Talk of the Town** Host, and wife Angela Chapman*

1   cup shortening
2   cups sugar
8   egg whites
4   cups flour
2   teaspoons baking powder
1   cup milk
1   teaspoon vanilla extract

▲ Cream the shortening and sugar in a mixer bowl until light and fluffy. Add the egg whites, 1 at a time, beating until the mixture forms thick peaks.

▲ Sift the flour and baking powder together twice. Add to the creamed mixture alternately with the milk, beating well after each addition. Stir in the vanilla. Pour into a greased and floured tube pan.

▲ Bake at 300 degrees for 1½ hours. May bake in a 2-inch sheet cake pan at 325 degrees for 35 minutes.

▲ Serve plain or with a white frosting, which will keep the cake from drying out.

Serves 10 to 15

Lelan's Fudge

Lelan A. Statom, NewsChannel 5 Meteorologist

3   cups chocolate chips
1   (14-ounce) can sweetened
    condensed milk
    Dash of salt
2   tablespoons vanilla extract
1   cup chopped nuts

▲ Combine the chocolate chips, sweetened condensed milk and salt in a heavy saucepan.

▲ Cook over low heat until the chocolate is melted, stirring constantly. Remove from the heat. Stir in the vanilla and nuts.

▲ Spread the mixture on a waxed-paper-lined baking sheet. Chill for several hours or until firm. Cut into squares to serve.

Serves 18 to 24

 Try these variations: Use white chocolate chips instead of milk chocolate or add toffee bits or marshmallows to the milk chocolate.

Chapter 2

Beverages and Appetizers

News Anchor Chris Clark joined
the NewsChannel 5 team in 1966.
For over 30 years Middle Tennesseans
have been tuning him in for the latest news.

NewsChannel 5

In 1979, NewsChannel 5 was the first Nashville station to use a helicopter in daily news coverage. "Copter Cam" is shown with the Nashville skyline as a backdrop.

"Night Train" was a popular show in the mid-1960s. This TV show was one of the first in the country to feature talented black musicians performing on a weekly basis and included artists like Jimi Hendrix, James Brown, Gladys Knight, BB King, Otis Redding, Wilson Pickett, Little Richard, and Joe Tex.

Buttermilk Blast

Nigel Olsson

3 cups buttermilk
1½ cups fruit juice
1 tablespoon sugar
Grapes and fruit slices

▲ Combine the buttermilk, fruit juice and sugar in a pitcher, stirring until the sugar dissolves.

▲ Place several grapes in the bottom of each glass. Pour in the mixture.

▲ Garnish with fruit slices.

Serves 4

Skinny Coffee Milkshake

Nigel Olsson

1 cup cold skim milk
3 ice cubes, crushed
1 teaspoon instant coffee powder
Artificial sweetener to taste

▲ Combine the skim milk, ice, coffee powder and artificial sweetener in a blender container.

▲ Process until smooth. Serve immediately.

Serves 1

5 Create a Strawberry Smoothie by processing ½ cup vanilla yogurt and 1 cup chopped strawberries in a blender until smooth. Pour into a chilled glass. Add some chilled ginger ale and stir gently.

International Coffees

Sue Ann Hemphill

Orange Coffee

½ cup instant coffee powder
¾ cup sugar
1 cup powdered coffee creamer
1½ teaspoons grated orange peel

▲ Process the coffee powder, sugar and coffee creamer in a blender until mixed. Store in an airtight container.

▲ To serve, add 3 heaping teaspoons of the mixture to a cup of hot water.

Serves 36

Mocha Coffee

½ cup instant coffee powder
1 cup powdered coffee creamer
2 tablespoons powdered cocoa
1 cup sugar

▲ Process the coffee powder, coffee creamer, cocoa and sugar in a blender until mixed. Store in an airtight container.

▲ To serve, add 3 heaping teaspoons of the mixture to a cup of hot water.

Serves 42

Cinnamon Coffee

½ cup instant coffee powder
⅔ cup sugar
⅔ cup powdered coffee creamer
½ teaspoon cinnamon

▲ Process the coffee powder, sugar, coffee creamer and cinnamon in a blender until mixed. Store in an airtight container.

▲ To serve, add 3 heaping teaspoons of the mixture to a cup of hot water.

Serves 28

Chilled Corn Chowder Page 47
Page 7

Captain John

Boiled Custard

Lynne Tolley, Miss Mary Bobo's Boarding House

2   quarts milk
6   large eggs
1½ cups sugar
2   teaspoons vanilla extract

▲ Warm the milk in a saucepan over low heat.

▲ Beat the eggs and sugar in a medium bowl. Add 1 cup of the warm milk gradually to the egg mixture, beating constantly. Pour the egg mixture into the warm milk, stirring constantly.

▲ Cook over low heat until the mixture thickens and coats the back of a spoon. Strain into a bowl. Stir in the vanilla.

▲ Chill, covered, until serving time.

▲ Ladle into punch cups. Garnish with Jack Daniel's Whiskey and a dollop of whipped cream.

Serves 16

Light Holiday Eggnog

Janet Chiavetta

1   teaspoon canola oil
1   cup egg substitute
¼   cup sugar
2   pints ice milk or fat-free ice cream, softened
1   teaspoon ground nutmeg

▲ Combine the oil, egg substitute and sugar in a large bowl. Beat with a wire whisk for 2 to 3 minutes.

▲ Add the ice milk and nutmeg, whisking until smooth. May add rum or brandy to taste.

▲ Serve immediately, or store in the refrigerator for several days until needed. For a thinner eggnog, add skim milk.

Serves 8

Lyric Springs Lemonade

Patsy Bruce, Lyric Springs Bed and Breakfast

2   cups sugar
2   cups water
10   sprigs of mint
    Juice of 12 lemons (2 cups)
2½ quarts water
6   to 8 lemon halves

▲ Combine the sugar, 2 cups water and mint in a saucepan. Bring to a boil. Cook until the sugar is dissolved and the liquid is clear and syrupy; cool. Remove the mint; discard.

▲ Mix the lemon juice, 2½ quarts water and 1 cup of the mint syrup in a 1-gallon pitcher, stirring well. Add lemon halves.

▲ Pour into tall glasses and garnish with sprigs of mint.

▲ To get the most juice from lemons or limes, microwave on 50% power for 1½ minutes, roll on a hard surface pressing firmly with palm of hand or soak the lemon in hot water for 10 minutes.

Serves 8 to 10

Peanut Butter and Jelly Punch

Nigel Olsson

4   cups milk
1   cup peanut butter
1   teaspoon vanilla extract
2   tablespoons jelly
1   pint chocolate ice cream, softened

▲ Combine the milk, peanut butter, vanilla, jelly and ice cream ½ at a time in a blender container.

▲ Process until the mixture is smooth. Pour into a large pitcher. Repeat with the remaining half of the ingredients.

▲ Serve immediately.

Serves 8 to 12

Baked Artichoke Dip

Ferris Robinson, The Gorgeless Gourmet

1 (12-ounce) can water-packed
   artichoke hearts, drained
½ cup fat-free mayonnaise
½ cup grated fat-free Parmesan
   cheese
1 clove garlic, minced
   Dash of Worcestershire sauce
   Pepper to taste

▲ Combine the artichoke hearts, mayonnaise, Parmesan cheese, garlic, Worcestershire sauce and pepper in a blender container.

▲ Process until the mixture is smooth. Pour into a baking dish sprayed with nonstick cooking spray.

▲ Bake at 350 degrees for 20 to 25 minutes.

▲ Serve with fat-free crackers.

Serves 6 to 8

 This is a great fat-free recipe!

Black Bean Layered Dip

Ann Cox, Kroger Food Stores

½ cup chopped green onions
12 ounces cream cheese, softened
2 tablespoons chopped fresh
   coriander, or 2 teaspoons dried
   coriander
1 clove garlic, minced
1 (15-ounce) can black beans,
   drained
2 tablespoons chopped fresh
   cilantro
1 (16-ounce) jar salsa
½ cup shredded Cheddar or
   Monterey Jack cheese
   Tortilla chips

▲ Reserve 1 tablespoon of the green onions for garnish. Combine the remaining green onions with the cream cheese, coriander and garlic in a large bowl; mix well.

▲ Spread over the bottom of an 8-inch baking dish or a 9-inch pie plate.

▲ Top with the black beans. Mix the cilantro with the salsa in a small bowl. Spread over the beans.

▲ Top with the cheese and reserved green onions. Serve with tortilla chips.

Serves 12 to 15

Mexican Strata

Doc Holliday

8 slices whole-grain bread, crusts trimmed

1½ cups shredded low-fat Cheddar cheese

1 (4-ounce) can chopped green chiles, drained

1 (2-ounce) jar sliced pimentos, drained

1⅓ cups skim milk

6 egg whites, or 1 cup egg substitute

¼ teaspoon cumin

▲ Spray an 8-inch square baking dish with nonstick cooking spray. Arrange 4 slices of the bread in the dish. Sprinkle with the cheese, green chiles and pimentos. Top with the remaining bread slices.

▲ Beat the milk, egg whites and cumin in a small bowl. Pour over the layers. Chill, covered, for 2 to 24 hours.

▲ Bake at 325 degrees for 60 to 75 minutes or until set and golden brown. Let stand 10 minutes before serving.

Serves 9

5 For a quick Cheesy Mexican Dip, serve a mixture of 1 cup each shredded Cheddar cheese and Velveeta cheese, one 6-ounce roll of garlic cheese and 1 can of Ro-Tel tomatoes in a chafing dish with tortilla chips.

TASTE OF **5** THE TOWN

Doc Holliday's Special Hot Mushroom Dip

Doc Holliday

4 slices bacon

8 ounces fresh mushrooms, sliced

1 medium onion, finely chopped

1 clove garlic, minced

2 tablespoons flour

½ teaspoon salt

⅛ teaspoon pepper

8 ounces cream cheese, cut into small pieces

2 teaspoons Worcestershire sauce

2 teaspoons soy sauce

½ cup sour cream

▲ Fry the bacon in a large skillet over medium heat until crispy. Remove the bacon to paper towels to drain. Drain the skillet, reserving 2 tablespoons of the pan drippings. Crumble the bacon and set aside.

▲ Sauté the mushrooms, onion and garlic in the reserved pan drippings over medium heat for 6 to 8 minutes or until tender and most of the liquid has evaporated. Stir in the flour, salt and pepper.

▲ Add the cream cheese, Worcestershire sauce and soy sauce. Cook over low heat until the cream cheese has melted, stirring constantly. Remove from the heat.

▲ Stir in the sour cream and crumbled bacon. Pour into a serving bowl.

▲ Serve warm with assorted crackers and breadsticks.

Serves 8 to 10

Chunky Vegetable Dip

Lynn Simmons

1 cup non-fat yogurt

1 (1-ounce) package vegetable soup mix

½ cup chopped vegetables of your choice

▲ Combine all ingredients in a bowl; mix well. Serve with crackers or vegetables.

Yield: 1½ cups

Baked Brie with Apple Chutney

Dianne Keenan, An Affair to Remember

½ cup unsalted butter

1½ cups packed light brown sugar

2 cups mixed dried fruit

½ cup golden raisins

6 ounces dried apple slices

1 (32-ounce) wheel Brie cheese

1 Granny Smith apple, sliced

1 Red Delicious apple, sliced
   Toasted sliced almonds

▲ Melt the butter in a large skillet over low heat. Add the brown sugar.

▲ Cook until the brown sugar is dissolved, stirring frequently. Add the mixed dried fruit, raisins and dried apple slices.

▲ Simmer for 5 minutes, stirring to coat the fruit.

▲ Place the cheese in an ovenproof chafing dish. Bake at 250 degrees just until melted. May cook in the microwave, but do not overcook.

▲ Pour the apple chutney over the cheese. Garnish with fresh apple slices and toasted almonds. Serve with crackers.

Serves 15 to 20

Easy Cheese Canapés

Ann Cox, Kroger Food Stores

2 cups shredded Cheddar cheese

½ cup chopped onion

⅓ cup chopped black olives

⅔ cup bacon bits

2 tablespoons chopped parsley

½ cup mayonnaise

24 slices party rye or pumpernickel bread

▲ Combine the cheese, onion, olives, bacon bits, parsley and mayonnaise in a bowl; mix well.

▲ Spread over the bread slices. Place on a baking sheet.

▲ Bake at 400 degrees for 5 minutes or until the cheese is melted. Serve immediately.

Serves 24

Chile Crab Egg Roll

Al Anderson, Jamaica Restaurant

1 tablespoon cream cheese
1 tablespoon crab meat
½ teaspoon chopped jalapeño with seeds
½ teaspoon chopped green onions
   Pinch of fresh minced garlic
2 drops of soy sauce
2 drops of lime juice
1 egg roll wrapper
   Egg wash
   Vegetable oil for deep-frying

▲ Combine the cream cheese, crab meat, jalapeño, green onions, garlic, soy sauce and lime juice in a small bowl. Mix thoroughly.

▲ Spoon the mixture over the egg roll wrapper, leaving a ½-inch border. Roll up the wrapper, folding in sides. Brush edge with egg wash to seal.

▲ Fry in 350-degree oil in a deep fryer at 350 degrees until golden brown; drain.

Serves 1

Fried Crab Won Tons

Doc Holliday

8 ounces cream cheese, softened
6 ounces frozen crab meat, thawed, drained
1 tablespoon prepared horseradish
½ teaspoon dried parsley, crumbled
½ teaspoon lemon juice
1 teaspoon garlic salt
½ teaspoon pepper
1 (12-ounce) package won ton wrappers
   Vegetable oil for deep-frying

▲ Mix the cream cheese, crab meat, horseradish, parsley, lemon juice and garlic salt in a medium bowl. Season with the pepper. Chill, covered, for 1 to 8 hours.

▲ Place 1 teaspoon of the crab meat filling in the center of each won ton wrapper. Brush the edges with water. Lift the corners of the wrapper over the filling to form a pouch, pressing to seal.

▲ Heat 1½ inches of oil to 350 degrees in a large heavy skillet.

▲ Fry the won tons in small batches for 1 to 2 minutes or until golden brown; drain. Serve hot.

Serves 50

Greek Pastries

Ferris Robinson, The Gorgeless Gourmet

1 (10-ounce) package frozen
    spinach, thawed, drained
1 medium onion, minced
5 egg whites, beaten
4 ounces feta cheese, crumbled
¾ cup cottage cheese
½ teaspoon salt
½ teaspoon pepper
½ teaspoon nutmeg
3 packages phyllo cups

▲ Mix the spinach, onion, egg whites, feta cheese, cottage cheese, salt, pepper and nutmeg in a medium bowl.

▲ Spoon an equal amount of the mixture into each phyllo cup. Place on a baking sheet.

▲ Bake at 350 degrees for 8 to 10 minutes or until bubbly.

Serves 15

Tortilla Bites

Ferris Robinson, The Gorgeless Gourmet

4 fat-free flour tortillas
1 onion, grated
1 (12-ounce) can black beans,
    drained
1 (8-ounce) jar chunky salsa

▲ Spray muffin cups with nonstick cooking spray. Cut each tortilla into quarters. Place tortilla quarters in the prepared muffin cups.

▲ Layer each tortilla with ½ teaspoon of the onion, 1 tablespoon of the black beans and 1 tablespoon of the salsa.

▲ Bake at 350 degrees for 8 to 10 minutes. Garnish with fat-free sour cream and chopped fresh cilantro. Serve hot.

Serves 16

Chapter 3

Soups and Salads

In 1969, CBS television purchased the show
Hee Haw, which was produced
at NewsChannel 5. The show became a network hit.

NewsChannel 5

Talk of the Town went on the air in 1984. Originally it was a 30-minute show hosted by Debbie Alan. Later, Harry Chapman and Joe Case joined the show and it was expanded to an hour. In 1995, Debbie Alan left the show and producer Meryll Rose became one of the hosts.

Talk of the Town's favorite cook, Doc Holliday, has prepared more recipes on the show than anyone else. He's been a "regular" since the first week. Host Meryll Rose has been a familiar face since 1995, when she became the newest host of *Talk of the Town*.

Corky's Fifteen-Bean Soup

Michael Attias, Corky's

1   (16-ounce) package dried
    15-bean mix
1   gallon water
1   tablespoon salt
1   teaspoon pepper
1   large onion, chopped
1   cup chopped carrots
1   cup chopped celery
2   cloves garlic, finely chopped
2   teaspoons chopped basil
1   bay leaf
2   tablespoons Worcestershire sauce
2   (14-ounce) cans whole tomatoes
8   ounces smoked turkey sausage
8   ounces smoked turkey, cubed
1½ tablespoons white vinegar

▲ Soak the beans in water to cover overnight. Fast soak methods will not work! Drain and rinse the beans.

▲ Place in an 8-quart soup pot with the water. Add the salt, pepper, onion, carrots, celery, garlic, basil, bay leaf, Worcestershire sauce and tomatoes.

▲ Cut the sausage into ¼-inch strips. Add the sausage and turkey to the soup pot. Stir with a large spoon to break up the tomatoes.

▲ Bring the mixture to a medium boil, stirring occasionally; cover. Reduce the heat to low. Simmer for 3 hours or until the beans are tender.

▲ Stir in the vinegar to cut the starchiness of the beans. Simmer for 15 to 20 minutes longer. Remove the bay leaf before serving.

Serves 6

Thirty-Minute Beef and Black Bean Soup

Terryl Propper, National Beef Cook-off, 1993

1   pound coarsely ground chuck
1   (11-ounce) can black bean soup
1   (15-ounce) can black beans,
    rinsed, drained
1⅓ cups water
1   cup prepared medium or hot
    chunky salsa
¼   cup thinly sliced green onions
¼   cup light sour cream

▲ Brown the ground chuck over medium heat in a large saucepan, stirring until crumbly and cooked through; drain well.

▲ Add the black bean soup, black beans, water and salsa. Bring to a boil; reduce the heat to low. Simmer, uncovered, for 15 minutes.

▲ Stir in the green onions; remove from the heat. Ladle into serving bowls. Top with sour cream. Garnish with sprigs of cilantro and serve with hot corn muffins.

Serves 4

Roasted Tomato and White Bean Soup

Lynda Ryan, Today's Gourmet

½ cup dried small white beans

3 cups defatted, reduced-sodium chicken stock

1½ teaspoons chopped fresh thyme, or ½ teaspoon dried thyme

2 pounds plum tomatoes, halved and seeded

5 cloves garlic, minced

1½ tablespoons olive oil

¼ cup dry vermouth

1 tablespoon chopped fresh sage, or 1 teaspoon dried sage

½ teaspoon sugar

Salt and freshly ground pepper to taste

▲ Place the beans in a large saucepan with water to cover by 1 inch over the top.

▲ Bring to a simmer over high heat; reduce the heat to low. Cook for 2 minutes.

▲ Remove from the heat and cover. Let stand for 1 hour. Drain and return to the saucepan. Add the chicken stock and thyme.

▲ Bring to a simmer; reduce the heat to low. Cook, covered, for 30 to 40 minutes or until the beans are tender.

▲ Arrange the tomato halves cut-side up in a 9x13-inch baking dish. Scatter the garlic over the tomatoes and drizzle with the olive oil.

▲ Bake for 1¼ to 1½ hours, brushing with the pan juices occasionally. The tomatoes will shrivel up and begin to brown. Remove from the oven and let stand to cool for 10 minutes. Remove and discard the peels. Chop 6 of the tomato halves and reserve.

▲ Place the remaining tomatoes in a blender container. Remove ¾ cup of the beans with a slotted spoon and add to the tomatoes with a small amount of the cooking liquid from the beans. Process until puréed. Pour back into the beans. Add the reserved tomatoes, vermouth, sage and sugar.

▲ Bring to a simmer. Cook for 3 minutes. Season with salt and pepper.

▲ May make up to 2 days ahead and store, covered, in the refrigerator.

Serves 4

Nancy and George Jones' Favorite Soup

Dixie and Tom T. Hall

1   pound dried navy beans
2   ribs celery, chopped
8   carrots, chopped
3   onions, chopped
1   (28-ounce) can stewed tomatoes
1   ham hock, or liquid smoke to taste
2   bay leaves
1   teaspoon minced dried rosemary
     Salt and pepper to taste

▲ Soak the beans in water to cover for 8 hours to overnight; drain well.

▲ Combine with the celery, carrots, onions, tomatoes, ham hock, bay leaves and rosemary in a large stockpot. Add enough water to cover generously.

▲ Bring to a boil; reduce the heat to low. Simmer for 3 hours or until the beans are tender, adding additional water if necessary. Season with salt and pepper. Remove the bay leaves before serving.

Serves 8

Cannellini and Crab Meat Soup

Sandro Bazzato, Antonio's Restaurant

1½ pounds cannellini (Italian white beans)
9   ounces crab meat
1   shallot, chopped
1   clove garlic, minced
     Salt, pepper and Tabasco sauce to taste
1   cup dry white chardonnay
2   quarts chicken stock
½   cup chopped parsley

▲ Soak the cannellini in water to cover for 8 hours to overnight; drain and rinse. Cook in a large saucepan with water to cover until the beans are tender; drain.

▲ Sauté the crab meat, shallot and garlic in a large saucepan for 3 to 5 minutes. Add the salt, pepper, Tabasco sauce, wine, chicken stock and parsley.

▲ Cook over medium heat until the sauce begins to thicken. Stir in the hot cooked cannellini.

Serves 6 to 8

Cream of Carrot Soup

Lynne Tolley, Miss Mary Bobo's Boarding House

3 tablespoons butter
5 to 6 carrots, peeled, thinly sliced
1 onion, thinly sliced
4 cups chicken stock
1½ tablespoons sugar
   Freshly ground pepper to taste
½ clove garlic, crushed with salt to taste
¾ cup heavy cream
¼ cup cooked rice

▲ Melt 2 tablespoons of the butter in a large saucepan. Add the carrots, onion and chicken stock.

▲ Simmer for 30 minutes or until the carrots are very tender. Drain, reserving the cooking liquid.

▲ Purée the carrots and onion in a food processor or blender. Return to the saucepan with the reserved cooking liquid. Stir in the sugar, pepper, garlic and cream.

▲ Bring to a boil; remove from the heat immediately. Whisk in the remaining 1 tablespoon butter. Garnish the servings with the rice.

Serves 4

Deep South Chicken Stew

Doreen Stewart, Stewart's Country Cupboard

1 medium onion, chopped
1 tablespoon vegetable oil
2 small ripe tomatoes, chopped
¾ teaspoon crumbled rosemary
1 cup defatted chicken broth
3 medium potatoes, quartered
½ cup frozen baby lima beans
¼ teaspoon pepper
1 (10-ounce) package frozen cut okra
½ cup frozen whole kernel corn
1¼ cups chopped cooked chicken

▲ Sauté the onion in the oil in a large saucepan until lightly browned. Add the tomatoes and rosemary.

▲ Cook over medium heat for 3 minutes, stirring frequently. Add the chicken broth, potatoes, lima beans and pepper.

▲ Bring to a boil; reduce the heat to low. Simmer for 10 minutes. Add the okra and corn.

▲ Cook, covered, for 10 minutes or until the vegetables are tender. Add the chicken. Cook until heated through.

Serves 4 to 6

Sunset Grill Basic Chili

Will Greenwood, Sunset Grill

1½ pounds chuck, cut into small
  pieces
  Salt and pepper to taste
2 tablespoons vegetable oil
1 onion, chopped
3 tablespoons chili powder
1 tablespoon ground cumin
2 tablespoons chopped garlic
3 tablespoons tomato paste
2 beef bouillon cubes
2½ cups water or beef stock

▲ Sprinkle the chuck with salt and pepper. Heat the oil in a large saucepan over medium-high heat. Add the chuck.

▲ Sauté the chuck until browned. Add the onion. Sweat the onion over low heat until it is translucent. Add the chili powder, cumin and garlic.

▲ Cook for 2 minutes over low heat. Add the tomato paste, bouillon cubes and water.

▲ Simmer over low heat for 2 hours, stirring occasionally.

▲ For a hearty variety, add one 16-ounce can pinto beans, 1 teaspoon cinnamon, 3 cups cooked polenta, 1 cup shredded cheese and ¼ cup minced red onion.

Serves 4 to 6

Black Bean Chili with Beer and Chipotle Peppers

Al Anderson, Pargo's

1 large onion, chopped
1 tablespoon minced garlic
1 cup olive oil
1 (16-ounce) bottle of dark beer
1 (16-ounce) can whole tomatoes,
  drained, puréed
1 can chipotle peppers
1 tablespoon ground cumin
¾ cup chili powder
2 cups chicken stock
2 tablespoons fresh lime juice
3 cups black beans, cooked
  Salt and pepper to taste

▲ Sauté the onion and garlic in the olive oil in a skillet until lightly browned. Add the beer.

▲ Cook until the liquid is reduced by half and the beer has evaporated. Add the tomatoes, chipotle peppers, cumin and chili powder.

▲ Cook for 10 minutes, stirring occasionally. Add the chicken stock, lime juice and black beans. Cook for 30 minutes longer. Season with salt and pepper.

▲ May also add cooked ground beef.

Serves 4 to 6

Barb Wire's Real Texas-Style Chili

Terri Cross, Barb Wire's Restaurant

2 pounds ground beef

1 green bell pepper, chopped

1 medium yellow onion, chopped

2 medium tomatoes, chopped

2 (14-ounce) cans chopped
    tomatoes

¼ cup catsup

5 tablespoons chili powder

¼ cup non-alcoholic beer

2 tablespoons sugar

⅓ cup jalapeño juice

1 tablespoon ground cumin

½ teaspoon oregano

1 teaspoon garlic powder

1 teaspoon salt

1 cup brewed coffee

▲ Brown the ground beef in a skillet, stirring until crumbly but slightly pink. Add the green pepper, onion and chopped fresh tomatoes. Cook until the ground beef is cooked through, stirring occasionally; drain well.

▲ Combine with the canned tomatoes, catsup, chili powder, beer, sugar, jalapeño juice, cumin, oregano, garlic powder, salt and coffee in a large stockpot.

▲ Bring to a boil; reduce the heat. Simmer for 1½ hours, stirring occasionally. Garnish with shredded cheese and whole jalapeños.

Serves 8

 Always make a double batch of chili and freeze half for a quick meal another week.

Chicken and White Bean Stew with Cilantro and Basil

*A Friend of **Talk of the Town***

1 large onion, chopped
1 clove garlic, finely chopped
¼ cup margarine or butter
4 cups chopped poached chicken
3 cups chicken broth
3 tablespoons chopped cilantro
1 tablespoon chopped fresh basil
2 teaspoons ground red chiles or cayenne
1 teaspoon ground cloves
1 cup chopped green tomatoes
4 cups cooked Great Northern beans
2 tablespoons ground cumin

▲ Sauté the onion and garlic in the margarine in a large stockpot until the onion is translucent. Add the chicken, chicken broth, cilantro, basil, ground chiles, cloves, green tomatoes, beans and cumin.

▲ Simmer over medium-low heat until heated through, stirring occasionally.

▲ Garnish with 4 green tomatoes, boiled and chopped, 3 tablespoons chopped cilantro, 2 green onions, sliced and 4 red tomatoes chopped.

Serves 4 to 6

Chilled Corn Chowder

*A Friend of **Talk of the Town***

1 bunch scallions
2 cups cooked whole kernel corn
  Juice of ½ lime or lemon
2 teaspoons fresh dill
  Salt and freshly ground pepper to taste
1 quart Bulgarian-style buttermilk or plain yogurt

▲ Slice the white part and 2 inches of the green part of the scallions. Place in a food processor container with the corn, lime juice, dill, salt and pepper.

▲ Process until smooth. Add 1 cup of the buttermilk. Process until well mixed.

▲ Pour into a bowl. Whisk in the remaining buttermilk. Chill thoroughly.

▲ Serve in frosted glasses or chilled cups, garnished with dill sprigs.

Serves 4 to 5

Crawfish Gumbo

Tom Overstreet, Mère Bulles

1   green bell pepper, chopped
1   red bell pepper, chopped
1   medium yellow onion, chopped
4   ribs celery, chopped
2   bay leaves
2   tablespoons chopped garlic
1   cup butter
2   tablespoons curry powder
1   teaspoon allspice
1   teaspoon cumin
2   teaspoons salt
1   teaspoon thyme
½   cup filé powder
1   cup flour
2   cups chopped tomatoes
2   cups puréed plum tomatoes
¼   cup Worcestershire sauce
1   tablespoon Tabasco sauce
3½   cups chicken stock
1   pound crawfish tails
2   cups chopped andouille sausage

▲ Sauté the bell peppers, onion, celery, bay leaves and garlic in the butter in a stockpot until the vegetables are tender. Stir in the curry powder, allspice, cumin, salt, thyme and filé powder. Dust with the flour. Add the chopped tomatoes, puréed tomatoes, Worcestershire sauce, Tabasco and chicken stock.

▲ Simmer for 10 minutes, stirring occasionally. Add the crawfish and andouille sausage.

▲ Simmer for 20 minutes longer, stirring frequently.

Serves 4 to 5

TASTE OF **5** THE TOWN

Louisiana Gumbo

Mindy Merrell, Tennessee Pride

¼ cup flour

¼ cup plus 1 tablespoon vegetable oil

1 pound mild or hot Tennessee Pride Italian sausage links, cut into 2-inch pieces

1 pound boneless, skinless chicken breasts, cut into 2-inch pieces

1 cup chopped onion

1 cup chopped celery with leaves

1 cup chopped green bell pepper

2 cloves garlic, minced

2 (14-ounce) cans chicken broth

1 (14-ounce) can whole tomatoes with juice, chopped

1 (10-ounce) package frozen sliced okra, thawed

1 teaspoon thyme

1 bay leaf

8 ounces fresh or frozen cooked shrimp, peeled

▲ Combine the flour and ¼ cup of the oil in a small skillet. Cook over low heat for 20 minutes or until the roux is a deep brown, stirring constantly. Remove from the heat and set aside.

▲ Brown the sausage in the remaining 1 tablespoon oil in a large stockpot. Remove the sausage with a slotted spoon and drain on paper towels, reserving the pan drippings.

▲ Brown the chicken in the reserved pan drippings. Remove the chicken with a slotted spoon and set aside.

▲ Add the onion, celery, green pepper and garlic to the pan drippings. Sauté for 5 minutes or until tender. Stir in the roux, mixing well. Add the chicken broth, tomatoes, okra, thyme, bay leaf, sausage, chicken and shrimp.

▲ Bring to a boil; reduce the heat. Simmer, covered, until the shrimp is cooked through. Remove the bay leaf. Serve over rice and garnish with chopped parsley.

Serves 6

Harvest Bisque

*A Friend of **Talk of the Town***

3 to 4 tablespoons butter, corn oil
   or peanut oil
1 large onion, chopped
3 to 4 cups chicken stock or
   vegetable stock
1 (28-ounce) can whole tomatoes
   with juice
1 tablespoon maple syrup or honey
4 cups pumpkin purée or butternut
   squash purée
   Salt to taste

▲ Melt the butter in a 10-inch skillet over medium-low heat. Add the onion. Sauté for 6 to 7 minutes or until tender but not browned. Add 3 cups of the stock. Simmer, partially covered, for 15 minutes.

▲ Pour the undrained tomatoes into a food processor container. Add the maple syrup. Process until puréed. Add the pumpkin and process for 1 minute. Strain the stock into a large saucepan, reserving the onion. Place the onion in a food processor container and process for 1 minute.

▲ Combine the puréed mixture with the stock in the saucepan. Season with salt. Simmer until very hot. Serve garnished with red pepper purée.

Serves 4 to 6

5 The flesh from smaller pumpkins will be sweeter and more tender than that from the larger species. One 5-pound pumpkin will yield about 4½ cups mashed, cooked pumpkin.

Caribbean Seafood Stew

Ken Gulley, Corporate Catering

1   teaspoon freshly chopped garlic

2   teaspoons freshly grated ginger

1   tablespoon chopped scallion

1   teaspoon chopped jalapeño

2   teaspoons olive oil

½   cup white wine

½   cup coconut milk

1   lobster tail

4   shrimp

6   mussels

8   ounces fish fillets

▲   Sauté the garlic, ginger, scallion and jalapeño in the olive oil in a large deep skillet for 1 to 2 minutes.

▲   Add the wine, coconut milk, lobster, shrimp, mussels and fish. Sauté for 4 to 5 minutes or until the fish flakes easily. Serve over beans and rice.

Serves 2

Shrimp Chowder

Red Lobster Restaurant

3   (10-ounce) cans condensed clam chowder

1½ cups milk

1½ cups half-and-half

½   cup clam juice

2   tablespoons melted butter

¼   teaspoon thyme

¼   cup sherry

1½ cups frozen corn

1   small Red Lobster Cocktail Shrimp Party Platter, tails removed

▲   Combine the clam chowder, milk, half-and-half, clam juice, butter, thyme, sherry and corn in a 4-quart saucepan.

▲   Cook over medium heat until hot but not boiling, stirring occasionally. Add the shrimp.

▲   Cook until heated through. Garnish with chopped chives and serve with crusty bread.

Serves 6

Spicy Southwestern Chowder

Diane Neahr, USA Rice Council

2 slices bacon, chopped

1 medium onion, chopped

1 cup shredded carrots

1 to 2 jalapeños, seeded, minced

2 cloves garlic, minced

1½ teaspoons chili powder

½ teaspoon ground cumin

3 cups low-fat milk

2 cups reduced-sodium chicken broth

3 cups cooked brown rice

1 (16-ounce) package frozen corn, or 1 (17-ounce) can corn, drained

6 large round sourdough rolls

▲ Fry the bacon over high heat in a large saucepan for 5 to 7 minutes or until crispy. Drain, reserving 1 tablespoon of pan drippings with the bacon in the saucepan.

▲ Add the onion, carrots, jalapeños, garlic, chili powder and cumin to the saucepan. Sauté for 3 to 5 minutes or until the onion is tender. Reduce the heat to medium. Add the milk, chicken broth, rice and corn.

▲ Simmer for 10 to 12 minutes or until the mixture begins to boil, stirring frequently. Cook for 1 minute longer; remove from the heat.

▲ Hollow out the rolls leaving a ½-inch "wall." Ladle the soup into the bread rounds. Garnish with chopped green onions.

Serves 6

5 When purchasing garlic, look for firm, plump bulbs with dry skins. Avoid heads with soft or shriveled cloves. Store fresh garlic in an open container in a cool dark place.

Caesar's Symphony Soup

Caesar Randazzo, Caesar's Restaurant

4   ounces chicken breast fillet
    Salt, pepper, oregano, basil and rosemary to taste
1   tablespoon butter
1   tablespoon freshly chopped parsley
1   tablespoon chopped onion
2   tablespoons chopped tomato
2   bay leaves
4   cups chicken broth
8   ounces meat-filled tortellini
1   egg, beaten
1   tablespoon grated Parmesan cheese

▲ Rinse the chicken and pat dry; cut into small pieces. Sprinkle the chicken with salt, pepper, oregano, basil and rosemary.

▲ Sauté the chicken in the butter in a skillet until lightly browned. Add the parsley, onion, tomatoes and bay leaves. Sauté until the onion is tender.

▲ Heat the chicken broth in a large saucepan. Add the tortellini. Cook over high heat for 2 to 3 minutes or until tender.

▲ Beat the egg with the Parmesan cheese, oregano and salt in a bowl. Whisk into the stock. Stir in the chicken mixture. Remove bay leaves. Season to taste and serve hot.

Serves 2 to 4

Stracciatella (Italian Egg Drop Soup)

Florine Johns, Nashville Herb Society

    Strained pan drippings from Roast Chicken with Herbs and White Wine (page 88)
1   quart water
2   eggs
2   tablespoons grated Parmesan or Romano cheese
1   tablespoon dried parsley flakes, or 2 tablespoons freshly chopped parsley

▲ Heat the pan drippings and water to the boiling point in a large saucepan.

▲ Beat the eggs with the cheese and parsley in a small bowl. Pour into the boiling broth slowly, whisking constantly.

▲ Simmer until the broth is clear. Serve with additional grated cheese.

▲ May use one 14-ounce can chicken broth instead of the pan drippings.

Serves 4

Fresh Strawberry Soup

Tammy Algood, Tennessee Agricultural Extension Service

2 cups sliced fresh strawberries
Juice of ½ lemon
1 cinnamon stick
2 cups water
Pinch of salt
¼ cup sugar
1 tablespoon cornstarch
2 tablespoons cold water
¼ cup heavy cream

▲ Combine the strawberries, lemon juice, cinnamon stick and 2 cups water in a saucepan. Bring to a boil; reduce the heat. Simmer for 10 minutes or until the berries are tender. Stir in the salt and sugar.

▲ Mix the cornstarch with the cold water in a small bowl until smooth. Stir into the strawberry mixture.

▲ Bring to a boil; reduce the heat. Simmer for 2 minutes. Remove from the heat and discard the cinnamon stick.

▲ Purée the mixture in a blender. Chill thoroughly. Stir in the cream just before serving. Serve in chilled glasses.

Serves 6

5 Choose brightly colored, plump strawberries that still have their green caps attached. One pint of fresh strawberries will yield about 2 cups of sliced strawberries.

Berry Cool Summer Salad

*A Friend of **Talk of the Town***

1½ cups California red and/or white grapes

¾ cup strawberries, hulled

¾ cup blueberries

½ cup apricot nectar

▲ Toss the grapes, strawberries, blueberries and apricot nectar in a medium bowl.

▲ Serve chilled or at room temperature.

Serves 4

Fat-Free Fruit Salad

Natoma Riley

1 (21-ounce) can juice-packed pineapple

1 (21-ounce) can peaches, drained

1 (10-ounce) package frozen unsweetened strawberries, thawed

4 bananas, sliced

1 small package sugar-free instant vanilla pudding mix

2 tablespoons powdered orange drink mix

▲ Combine the undrained pineapple, peaches, strawberries, bananas, pudding mix and orange drink mix in a large bowl. Toss gently to mix.

▲ Serve as a fruit salad, or over fat-free yogurt.

Serves 12 to 16

Fresh Fruit Salad

Tammy Algood, Tennessee Agricultural Extension Service

1   cup chopped plums
1   cup sliced peaches
1   cup sliced kiwifruit
1   cup chopped pears
1   cup raspberries
2   tablespoons flour
½   cup packed brown sugar
½   cup butter
1   cup white wine or cooking sherry
½   cup chopped pecans

▲ Layer the plums, peaches, kiwifruit, pears and raspberries in a buttered medium baking dish.

▲ Combine the flour, brown sugar, butter and wine in the top of a double boiler. Cook over boiling water until smooth and thickened, stirring frequently. Pour over the fruit layers. Top with the pecans. Chill in the refrigerator for 8 hours to overnight.

▲ Bake at 350 degrees for 10 to 15 minutes or until bubbly. Serve hot.

Serves 6

Fruit Blizzard

Doc Holliday

1½ cups Thompson seedless grapes
1½ cups red seedless grapes
2   cups nonfat sour cream
    Juice of 2 limes
½   cup packed brown sugar
1   tablespoon ground ginger

▲ Combine the grapes, sour cream, lime juice, brown sugar and ginger in a bowl and mix gently. Chill thoroughly.

▲ Serve in chilled glass dishes garnished with a wedge of lime and a slice of kiwifruit.

Serves 4 to 6

Sweet and Savory Broccoli Salad

Lynne Tolley, Miss Mary Bobo's Boarding House

1   cup mayonnaise

2   tablespoons apple cider vinegar

½   cup sugar

    Florets from 1 large head broccoli

¼   cup chopped red onion

½   cup raisins

½   cup chopped pecans

8   ounces bacon, crisp-fried, crumbled

½   cup sunflower seeds

▲ Whisk the mayonnaise, vinegar and sugar together in a small bowl.

▲ Combine with the broccoli florets, onion, raisins and pecans in a medium bowl, tossing to coat. Chill for several hours to overnight.

▲ Top with the bacon and sunflower seeds before serving.

Serves 4 to 6

Warm Broccoli Mushroom Salad

*Nathalie Dupree, **Nathalie Dupree Cooks Quick Meals for Busy Days***

1   head broccoli, or 1 (12-ounce) package frozen broccoli florets

3   slices bacon, chopped

1   medium onion, finely chopped

2   tablespoons raspberry or balsamic vinegar

8   ounces mushrooms

▲ Cut the broccoli into bite-sized pieces. Steam until tender-crisp. Rinse with cold water and set aside to drain.

▲ Fry the bacon in a skillet until browned. Add the onion. Cook for 2 to 3 minutes longer or until the bacon is crispy and the onion is tender. Add the raspberry vinegar.

▲ Bring to a boil. Cook until the mixture is reduced by half; remove from the heat.

▲ Add the broccoli and mushrooms, tossing to coat. Serve immediately.

Serves 4 to 6

Tangy Lemon Coleslaw

Doc Holliday

½ cup mayonnaise

¼ cup fresh lemon juice

2 tablespoons olive oil

1 tablespoon white vinegar

1 teaspoon salt

½ teaspoon pepper

½ cup sour cream

2 tablespoons Dijon mustard

2 tablespoons sugar

1 tablespoon prepared horseradish

½ teaspoon celery seeds

8 cups shredded cabbage

½ red bell pepper, cut into strips

½ green bell pepper cut into strips

¼ red onion, cut into strips

1 carrot, shredded

2 tablespoons freshly chopped parsley

2 teaspoons grated lemon peel

▲ Whisk the mayonnaise, lemon juice, olive oil, vinegar, salt, pepper, sour cream, mustard, sugar, horseradish and celery seeds in a medium bowl until blended. Chill for several hours to overnight.

▲ Combine the cabbage, bell peppers, onion, carrot, parsley and lemon peel in a large bowl. Add the mayonnaise mixture to taste, tossing to coat. Serve chilled.

Serves 6

TASTE OF **5** THE TOWN

Layered Corn Bread Salad

Ann Cox, Kroger Food Stores

1   (6-ounce) package corn bread or jalapeño corn bread mix
    Pinch of sage
1   (4-ounce) can chopped green chiles, drained
2   (16-ounce) cans pinto beans, drained, rinsed
2   (16-ounce) cans whole kernel corn, drained
½   cup chopped green bell peppers
½   cup chopped green onions
3   large tomatoes, chopped
2   cups shredded Cheddar cheese
1   envelope ranch salad dressing mix
1   cup sour cream
1   cup mayonnaise
10 slices bacon, crisp-fried, crumbled

▲ Prepare the corn bread using package directions, adding sage and green chiles. Bake, cool and coarsely crumble.

▲ Combine the pinto beans and corn in a small bowl. Mix the green peppers and green onions in a small bowl.

▲ Layer the corn bread crumbs, bean mixture, tomatoes, green pepper mixture and cheese ½ at a time in an 8x13-inch dish.

▲ Mix the dressing mix, sour cream and mayonnaise in a bowl until smooth. Spread over the layers. Top with the crumbled bacon. Chill for 8 hours to overnight before serving.

Serves 12

Cucumber and Tomato Salad

A Friend of **Talk of the Town**

1	cucumber
1	large tomato
½	teaspoon non-iodized salt
1	tablespoon sugar
1	tablespoon cider vinegar
1	teaspoon sesame oil

▲ Peel the cucumber and cut lengthwise into 4 strips; remove the seeds. Cut the strips into ¾-inch pieces.

▲ Pour boiling water over the tomato in a bowl and let stand for 1 minute. Rinse with cold water and peel. Cut into sections and remove the seeds. Cut into ¾-inch pieces.

▲ Toss the tomato, cucumber and salt in a bowl. Chill in the refrigerator.

▲ Combine the sugar, vinegar and oil in a small bowl, mixing well. Pour over the cucumber mixture, tossing to coat. Serve cold.

▲ May substitute radish or celery slices for the cucumber and tomato. If using a Japanese cucumber, also called English, Hothouse, Burpless or seedless cucumber, do not peel.

Serves 2

Gazpacho Salad

A Friend of **Talk of the Town**

4	large tomatoes
2	cucumbers, peeled, chopped
1	green bell pepper, chopped
1	red onion, chopped
⅓	cup red wine vinegar
⅓	cup tomato sauce
½	cup olive oil
1	teaspoon lemon juice
	Salt and pepper to taste

▲ Peel and chop the tomatoes, reserving a 6-inch strip of the peel for garnish.

▲ Arrange the tomatoes, cucumbers, green pepper and onion in separate sections on a serving plate. Roll the reserved tomato peel into a rose shape, securing with a wooden pick. Place in the center of the vegetables.

▲ Mix the vinegar, tomato sauce, olive oil and lemon juice in a small bowl. Sprinkle with salt and pepper. Pour over the vegetables. Garnish with croutons.

Serves 6

Grilled Summer Salad

Randy Rayburn, Sunset Grill

¼ cup balsamic vinegar or lemon juice

2 tablespoons olive oil

2 tablespoons water

½ tablespoon freshly chopped basil or parsley

1 clove garlic, minced

1 Vidalia or sweet onion, sliced

1 tomato, sliced

1 pineapple, sliced

1 squash or zucchini, sliced

8 ounces mixed salad greens

Salt and pepper to taste

▲ Whisk the vinegar, oil, water, basil and garlic together in a small bowl.

▲ Arrange the onion, tomato, pineapple and squash in a large shallow dish. Pour the marinade mixture over the vegetable mixture and let stand for 30 to 60 minutes. Drain, reserving the marinade.

▲ Place the vegetable mixture over medium hot coals. Grill for 2 to 3 minutes on each side.

▲ Drizzle the reserved marinade over the salad greens. Top with the grilled vegetable mixture. Season with salt and pepper.

Serves 2 to 4

5 For a summer deck party, offer crisp salad greens in a large bowl surrounded by "salad fixings" in small glass flowerpots.

Duck and Warm Brie Salad

Jody Faison, Faison Restaurant Group

½ medium head endive, torn

½ medium head iceberg lettuce, torn

½ medium head romaine lettuce, torn

Garlic croutons

¼ cup olive oil

2 teaspoons minced shallots

1 teaspoon minced garlic

¼ cup sherry wine vinegar

1 tablespoon fresh lemon juice

2 teaspoons Dijon mustard

5 ounces ripe Brie cheese, cut into pieces, at room temperature

½ cup shredded roast duck

Freshly ground pepper to taste

▲ Toss the lettuce and croutons in a large bowl; set aside.

▲ Heat the olive oil over medium-low heat in a saucepan for 10 minutes. Add the shallots and garlic. Sauté for 5 minutes or until translucent.

▲ Whisk in the vinegar, lemon juice and mustard. Add the cheese and duck.

▲ Cook over very low heat until the cheese is melted, stirring constantly. Season with pepper.

▲ Pour the warm mixture over the lettuce, tossing gently to coat. Serve immediately.

Serves 4 to 6

5 Coring a head of lettuce with a knife causes the surrounding area to discolor more quickly. Leave core intact or remove by striking core end on kitchen counter and twisting out core with fingers.

Panzanella

Terry Carr-Hall, Provençe

1   pound dry Tuscan dark bread, cut into cubes
2   large tomatoes
1   large red onion
8   to 10 basil leaves
    Salt and pepper to taste
½   cup virgin olive oil
1   tablespoon wine vinegar

▲ Soak the bread in very cold water with the whole tomatoes, onion and basil leaves.

▲ Squeeze the bread to remove all the liquid; place in a large plastic container.

▲ Cut the onion into quarters and finely slice. Arrange the onion over the bread.

▲ Tear the basil leaves into ½-inch pieces. Place over the onion. Chop the tomatoes into ½-inch pieces; layer over the basil. Chill, covered, for 2 hours or longer.

▲ Whisk the salt, pepper, olive oil and vinegar together in a small bowl. Pour over the layers; toss to coat. Serve immediately.

Serves 6

5 Purchase tomatoes that are firm, well-shaped, richly colored and noticeably fragrant. Store ripe tomatoes stem side down at room temperature away from direct sunlight and use within a few days.

Pizza Pasta Salad Supreme

Carey Clarke Aron, The Pasta Shoppe

12 ounces pasta

1 medium green bell pepper, chopped

1 medium red bell pepper, chopped

4 to 6 green onions, sliced

1 (2-ounce) can sliced black olives, drained

3 ounces pepperoni slices, cut into quarters

1 large tomato, chopped

1 (4-ounce) can sliced mushrooms, drained

4 ounces Italian salad dressing

½ cup mayonnaise

1 teaspoon dried oregano

½ teaspoon salt

¼ teaspoon pepper

2 cloves garlic, minced

1 teaspoon fennel seeds

2 tablespoons grated Parmesan cheese

1 cup shredded mozzarella cheese

▲ Cook the pasta using package directions. Drain and rinse the pasta with cold water.

▲ Combine the pasta with bell peppers, green onions, olives, pepperoni, tomato and mushrooms in a large bowl, tossing gently.

▲ Whisk the salad dressing, mayonnaise, oregano, salt, pepper, garlic and fennel seeds in a small bowl. Pour over the pasta mixture; toss to coat.

▲ Add the Parmesan cheese and mozzarella cheese; toss well. Serve immediately.

Serves 8 to 10

Al's Shrimp and Crab Pasta Salad

Al Anderson, Santa Fe Restaurant

8   ounces penne pasta

¼   cup olive oil

2   teaspoons balsamic vinegar

2   teaspoons Dijon mustard

½   teaspoon ground cumin

1   teaspoon minced garlic

½   teaspoon sugar

½   teaspoon salt

3   dashes of hot pepper sauce

½   teaspoon curry sauce

2   large tomatoes, seeded and chopped

⅔   cup chopped green bell pepper

⅔   cup chopped red bell pepper

1   (5-ounce) can sliced water chestnuts, drained

½   cup sliced green onions

½   cup freshly chopped mint

½   cup chopped red onion

4   teaspoons orange juice

5   ounces small shrimp, cooked, sliced

5   ounces crab meat, or imitation crab meat

▲ Cook the pasta using package directions. Drain and rinse with cold water; set aside.

▲ Combine the olive oil, vinegar, mustard, cumin, garlic, sugar, salt, pepper sauce and curry sauce in a small bowl. Whisk until smooth.

▲ Mix the tomatoes, bell peppers, water chestnuts, green onions, mint, onion, orange juice, shrimp and crab meat in a large bowl. Pour the dressing over the mixture, tossing to coat.

▲ Add the pasta, tossing well. Serve chilled.

Serves 6 to 8

Southwestern Pasta Salad

*Holly Clegg, **Trim and Terrific American Favorites***

½ teaspoon ground cumin

1 (28-ounce) can tomatoes, puréed

1 onion, chopped

1½ teaspoons chili powder

1 teaspoon dried oregano

½ teaspoon minced garlic

½ teaspoon sugar

¼ teaspoon ground cinnamon

¼ teaspoon red pepper flakes
   Salt and pepper to taste

16 ounces rotini pasta

1 (16-ounce) can black beans,
   drained

1 (10-ounce) package frozen corn

1 (4-ounce) can chopped green
   chiles

▲ Heat a large saucepan sprayed with nonstick cooking spray over medium heat. Add the cumin. Cook for 1 minute, stirring constantly.

▲ Add the tomato purée, onion, chili powder, oregano, garlic, sugar, cinnamon, red pepper flakes, salt and pepper.

▲ Bring the mixture to a boil; reduce the heat. Simmer, covered, for 20 to 25 minutes.

▲ Cook the pasta using package directions, but omitting the oil and salt. Drain well. Cover to keep warm.

▲ Stir the black beans, corn and green chiles into the tomato mixture. Cook for 5 minutes or until the corn is tender-crisp; remove from the heat.

▲ Pour over the pasta in a large bowl, tossing to coat. Garnish with shredded reduced-fat Cheddar cheese.

Serves 6 to 8

Three-Pepper Rice Salad

Sharon McComb, Watertown Bed and Breakfast

2½ cups water

1 cup uncooked rice

1 tablespoon chicken-flavored instant bouillon, or 3 chicken bouillon cubes

1 (15-ounce) can dark red kidney beans, drained

1 cup chopped jicama

1 cup chopped green bell pepper

1 cup chopped red bell pepper

1 (4-ounce) can chopped green chiles

⅓ cup lemon juice

3 tablespoons vegetable oil

2 teaspoons sugar

1½ teaspoons ground cumin

¼ teaspoon garlic powder

▲ Combine the water, rice and chicken bouillon in a medium saucepan. Bring to a boil; reduce the heat. Simmer, covered, for 15 to 20 minutes or until the liquid is absorbed.

▲ Toss the kidney beans, jicama, bell peppers and green chiles together in a medium bowl. Stir in the rice.

▲ Whisk the lemon juice, oil, sugar, cumin and garlic powder in a small bowl until smooth. Pour over the rice mixture.

▲ Chill, covered, for 2 to 4 hours. Stir and serve over a bed of lettuce.

Serves 6 to 8

Southwest Salad

Charlie Lico and Rebecca Holden, Carnton Symphony on the Lawn

1   yellow onion, chopped

2   to 3 tablespoons olive oil

2   (14-ounce) cans chicken broth

2   cups packaged saffron rice

1   cup long-grain white rice

2   (16-ounce) cans black beans, drained

2   to 3 cups yellow kernel corn

4   to 5 green onions, chopped

⅔   cup vegetable oil

¼   cup fresh lime juice

2   tablespoons cider vinegar

2   tablespoons brown sugar

2   teaspoons chili powder

2   teaspoons ground cumin

1   jalapeño, chopped, seeded (optional)

▲ Sauté the onion in the olive oil in a large saucepan until the onion is translucent. Combine the chicken broth with enough water to measure 3 cups of liquid. Add to the sautéed onion.

▲ Bring to a boil. Add the saffron rice and white rice; reduce the heat. Simmer until all the liquid is absorbed.

▲ Combine the rice, black beans, corn and green onions in a large bowl, tossing to mix.

▲ Process the vegetable oil, lime juice, vinegar, brown sugar, chili powder, cumin and jalapeño in a food processor until smooth. Pour over the rice mixture, tossing to coat.

▲ Chill, covered, for up to 2 days. Serve heated or at room temperature. Garnish with cilantro.

Serves 6 to 8

Chapter 4

Vegetables and Sides

In 1974 NewsChannel 5 hired the first female co-anchor in the Nashville market. Oprah Winfrey went on the air with Harry Chapman.

NewsChannel **5**

In 1958 NewsChannel 5 debuted weather radar. For 14 years NewsChannel 5 was the ONLY Nashville station to provide radar in its weather presentation.

In 1955 NewsChannel 5 was the first Nashville station to hire a female weatherperson. Jean Hughes delivered the weather, complete with weather symbols constructed of styrofoam, hatpins and toothpicks.

Sliced Baked Potatoes

GREAT AMERICAN RECIPES

Potatoes, Pasta and Rice   Card **11**

Group **10**

Preparation time: 15 min.
Baking time: 1 hr.

Oven temperature: 425°F

Microwave cooking: see other side

This is a very easy way to give the bland potato a lot of new flavor. The light

EASY & TASTY

For 4 servings you will need:

4 medium even potatoes
1 tsp. salt
2 to 3 Tbsp. melted butter
2 to 3 Tbsp. chopped fresh herbs such as parsley, chives, thyme or sage or
2 to 3 tsp. dried herbs of your choice
4 Tbsp. grated Cheddar cheese
1½ Tbsp. Parmesan cheese

Preparation:

1 Peel potatoes if the skin is tough, otherwise just scrub and rinse them.

2 Cut potatoes into thin slices but not all the way through. Use a handle of a spoon to prevent knife from cutting all the way.

3 Put potatoes in a baking dish. Fan them slightly.

4 Sprinkle with salt and drizzle with butter. Sprinkle with herbs.

5 Bake potatoes at 425°F for about 50 minutes.

6 Remove from oven. Sprinkle with cheeses.

7 Bake potatoes for another 10 to 15 minutes until lightly browned, cheeses are melted and potatoes are soft inside. Check with a fork.

Tips:

You may use caraway seeds or cumin in place of herbs, if desired. Use about 1½ tsp. for 4 large potatoes.

Good served with:

Any meat, fish or poultry dishes or as a main dish with just a salad.

How to Microwave
Sliced Baked Potatoes

Microwave setting .... HIGH 100%
Microwave cooking time .... 14 to 16 min.

For 4 servings you will need:

- 4 medium even potatoes
- 1 tsp. salt
- 2 to 3 Tbsp. melted butter
- 2 to 3 Tbsp. chopped fresh herbs such as parsley, chives, thyme or sage or
- 2 to 3 tsp. dried herbs of your choice
- 4 Tbsp. grated Cheddar cheese
- 1½ Tbsp. Parmesan cheese

Preparation:

1 Peel potatoes if the skin is tough, otherwise just rinse and pat dry.

2 Cut potatoes into thin slices but not all the way through. Use a handle of a spoon to prevent knife from cutting all the way.

3 Place potatoes in a microsafe dish or pan. Sprinkle with melted butter and chopped parsley, chives or sage.

4 Microwave at HIGH power for 10 minutes, rearranging the potatoes after 5 minutes.

5 Let rest for 5 minutes.

6 Sprinkle with grated cheese and Parmesan cheese.

7 Microwave for another 4 to 6 minutes at HIGH power until cheeses are melted and potatoes are soft. Sprinkle with salt.

8 Serve potatoes as a side dish or as a main dish with just a salad.

PER SERVING		PERCENTAGE OF USRDA	
Calories	235	Protein	8.7%
Protein	5.6 g	Calcium	9.2%
Fat	8.8 g	Iron	4.0%
Carbohydrates	33.2 g	Vitamin A	8.1%
Sodium	732 mg	Vitamin C	35.5%

Baked Bean Combo

Carolyn Sager, Potluck Contest Winner

8   slices bacon, chopped
2   large onions, chopped
1   cup packed brown sugar
1   teaspoon powdered mustard
½   teaspoon garlic powder
1   teaspoon salt
½   cup cider vinegar
2   (16-ounce) cans Great Northern beans
1   (16-ounce) can lima beans
1   (16-ounce) can red kidney beans
1   (28-ounce) can pork and beans

▲ Fry the bacon and onions in a skillet until the bacon is crumbly and the onions are tender; drain.

▲ Combine with the brown sugar, mustard, garlic powder, salt and vinegar in a large saucepan. Drain all the beans. Stir into the mixture.

▲ Cook over low heat for 2 hours, stirring occasionally.

Serves 14 to 16

Cabbage Casserole

Doreen Stewart, Stewart Country Cupboard

1   pound ground beef or ground turkey
    Garlic seasoning to taste
1   (10-ounce) can cream of celery soup
1   medium head cabbage, shredded
1   onion, chopped
1   rib celery, chopped
1   to 2 cups shredded Cheddar cheese
½   to 1 cup dried bread crumbs

▲ Brown the ground beef in a skillet, stirring until crumbly; drain. Stir in the garlic seasoning and the soup.

▲ Alternate layers of the cabbage, onion, celery, beef mixture and cheese in a large baking dish until all ingredients are used. Top with bread crumbs.

▲ Bake at 350 degrees for 1 hour. Garnish with paprika and parsley.

Serves 4 to 6

Bean-Stuffed Cabbage Rolls

Doc Holliday

1 large head cabbage (about 3 pounds), core removed

¼ cup chopped onion

2 teaspoons chopped fresh sage, or ½ teaspoon dried sage

¼ teaspoon cumin

1 clove garlic, finely chopped

1 tablespoon reduced-calorie margarine

½ cup shredded carrot

1 (15-ounce) can black beans, drained

½ cup vegetable or chicken broth

½ cup skim milk

2 teaspoons cornstarch

¼ teaspoon salt

1 teaspoon chopped fresh sage, or ¼ teaspoon dried sage

6 tablespoons shredded low-fat Swiss cheese

▲ Place the cabbage in a bowl and cover with warm water. Let stand for 10 minutes or until the leaves loosen slightly. Remove 12 of the leaves. Cover with boiling water. Let stand, covered, for 10 minutes or until the leaves are limp; drain. Shred 1½ cups of the remaining cabbage and set aside.

▲ Cook the onion, 2 teaspoons sage, cumin and garlic in the margarine in a 2-quart nonstick saucepan for 3 minutes or until the onion is tender, stirring frequently. Stir in the shredded cabbage, carrot and the black beans.

▲ Spoon a scant ¼ cup of the bean mixture on the stem end of a cabbage leaf. Roll up, tucking in sides. Repeat with the remaining leaves.

▲ Place the cabbage rolls seam side down in an ungreased 9x13-inch baking dish. Pour the vegetable broth over the rolls.

▲ Bake, covered, at 350 degrees for 30 to 35 minutes or until heated through. Remove the rolls with a slotted spoon and keep warm.

▲ Drain the liquid from the baking dish, reserving ½ cup. Pour the milk into a saucepan. Add the cornstarch, stirring until smooth. Add the reserved cooking liquid, salt and 1 teaspoon sage. Bring to a boil over medium heat, stirring constantly. Cook for 1 minute.

▲ Arrange the cabbage rolls on a serving plate. Cover with the sauce and top with the cheese.

Serves 6

Corn Pudding

Ann Cox, Kroger Food Stores

½   cup chopped green onions
½   cup chopped green bell pepper
½   cup chopped red bell pepper
3   tablespoons flour
½   teaspoon seasoned salt
¼   teaspoon pepper
1   (12-ounce) can evaporated skim milk
2   eggs, beaten
    Kernels of 6 ears of fresh corn

▲ Sauté the green onions and bell peppers in a large skillet sprayed with nonstick cooking spray until tender crisp. Stir in the flour, salt and pepper.

▲ Add the evaporated milk gradually, stirring over low heat until the mixture is thickened. Stir a small portion of the mixture into the eggs in a small bowl. Pour the egg mixture into the skillet, beating well. Remove from the heat.

▲ Add the corn. Pour into a 2-quart baking dish sprayed with nonstick cooking spray.

▲ Bake at 350 degrees for 35 to 40 minutes or until set.

Serves 8 to 10

Shoe Peg Corn Casserole

Jan Howard, Grand Ole Opry Star

1   (16-ounce) can French-cut green beans, drained
1   (16-ounce) package frozen Shoe Peg corn, thawed
1   (10-ounce) can cream of mushroom soup
1   cup sour cream
    Salt and pepper to taste
1   tube butter crackers, crushed
½   cup margarine, melted

▲ Spoon the green beans into a 2-quart microwave-safe baking dish.

▲ Mix the corn, soup and sour cream in a bowl. Season with salt and pepper. Spoon over the green beans.

▲ Sprinkle with the cracker crumbs and drizzle with the melted margarine.

▲ Microwave on Medium for 8 to 15 minutes or until bubbly.

Serves 4 to 6

Country-Style Sautéed Green Beans

David Swett, Jr., Swett's Restaurant

1   pound fresh green beans, trimmed and snapped

1   slice center-cut country ham, chopped

1   medium yellow onion, chopped

1   medium green bell pepper, chopped

1   medium red bell pepper, chopped

½   teaspoon minced fresh garlic

¼   cup butter

1   teaspoon sugar

    Salt and pepper to taste

▲ Blanch the green beans in boiling water for 1 to 2 minutes. Drain and plunge into ice water for a few seconds; drain.

▲ Sauté the ham, onion, bell peppers and garlic in the butter in a large skillet for 3 to 4 minutes. Add the green beans.

▲ Cook until heated through. Season with the sugar, salt and pepper.

Serves 4

5 Select fresh green beans that have firm, smooth, brightly colored pods. They may be stored in an airtight sealable plastic bag in the refrigerator for up to 4 days. Rinse the green beans just before using.

Lima Bean Risotto

Doc Holliday

3   tablespoons butter

1   small onion, chopped

2   fresh rosemary sprigs, or 1½
    teaspoons dried crumbled
    rosemary

3   (14-ounce) cans chicken broth

1½ cups water

2¼ cups arborio rice

¾   cup dry white wine

1½ (10-ounce) packages frozen baby
    lima beans, thawed

1¼ cups grated Parmesan cheese
    Salt and pepper to taste

▲ Melt the butter in a medium heavy saucepan over medium heat. Add the onion and rosemary. Cook for 8 minutes or until the onion is translucent, stirring occasionally.

▲ Simmer the chicken broth with the water in a medium saucepan. Reduce the heat to low; cover and keep warm.

▲ Stir the rice into the onion mixture. Cook for 2 minutes. Add the wine. Cook until all the liquid is absorbed, stirring frequently.

▲ Add the lima beans and ¾ cup of the broth mixture. Simmer over low heat until the liquid is absorbed, stirring frequently.

▲ Cook for 20 minutes or until the rice is tender but firm, adding the remaining broth mixture ½ cup at a time and stirring frequently and cooking until the liquid is absorbed before the next addition. Remove from the heat.

▲ Stir in the Parmesan cheese and season with salt and pepper.

Serves 6

 Arborio, an Italian short grain rice, is available at Italian markets as well as specialty food stores. Medium grain rice can be substituted.

Baked Vidalia Onions

Jack Favier, Executive Chef, Baptist Hospital

6 medium Vidalia onions
2 teaspoons Dijon mustard
2 teaspoons honey
2 teaspoons Balsamic vinegar
1 teaspoon Mrs. Dash seasoning
1 teaspoon pepper
2 teaspoons olive oil

▲ Peel the onions, cutting off the ends; rinse in water. Cut a deep star in the top of each onion, cutting halfway through. Place on a baking sheet.

▲ Combine the mustard, honey, vinegar, seasoning and pepper in a small bowl. Add the olive oil slowly, stirring constantly. Spoon half of the mixture over the onions.

▲ Bake at 350 degrees for 20 minutes. Spoon the remaining mustard mixture over the onions. Bake for 20 minutes longer or until golden brown.

▲ Arrange on a serving plate. Garnish with chopped parsley or paprika.

Serves 6

Family Reunion Onion Casserole

Doc Holliday

3 medium sweet white onions, sliced
8 ounces mushrooms, sliced
2 tablespoons butter
1 cup shredded Monterey Jack and Colby cheese
1 (10-ounce) can cream of mushroom soup
1 (5-ounce) can evaporated milk
2 teaspoons soy sauce
6 to 8 (½-inch-thick) slices French bread
6 to 8 thin slices Swiss cheese

▲ Sauté the onions and mushrooms in the butter in a large skillet over medium-high heat. Spoon into a 2-quart baking dish. Sprinkle with the shredded cheese.

▲ Combine the soup, evaporated milk and soy sauce in a small bowl. Pour over the onion mixture.

▲ Arrange the bread slices over the layers. Top with Swiss cheese. Chill, covered, for 4 hours to overnight.

▲ Bake, loosely covered, at 375 degrees for 30 minutes. Bake, uncovered, for 15 to 20 minutes longer or until heated through.

▲ Let stand for 5 minutes before serving.

Serves 6 to 8

Gourmet Potato Pancakes

Doc Holliday

2¼ pounds russet potatoes, peeled,
   cut into 1-inch cubes
1½ cups shredded Cheddar cheese
¼ cup unsalted butter, softened
¼ cup sour cream
4 ounces bacon, crisp-fried,
   crumbled
2 green onions, chopped
¾ teaspoon salt
¼ teaspoon white pepper
   Vegetable oil for frying

▲ Place the potatoes in a large saucepan with cold water to cover. Bring to a boil. Cook for 20 minutes or until the potatoes are tender. Drain well, place in a mixer bowl and let cool for 3 minutes.

▲ Beat the potatoes at medium speed until smooth. Add the cheese, butter, sour cream, bacon, green onions, salt and pepper, stirring well. Refrigerate until completely chilled or overnight.

▲ Shape ⅓ cup of the potato mixture into a 3-inch round. Repeat with the remaining mixture. Place on a waxed-paper-lined tray, separating layers with waxed paper. Chill for 1 hour.

▲ Heat the oil in a large heavy skillet. Cook the potato pancakes for 3 minutes on each side or until golden brown. Transfer to warmed plates. Serve immediately.

Serves 8

Sweetheart Potatoes

Penny Deweese, Miss Penny's

1 pound baking potatoes, peeled,
   thickly sliced
½ cup melted butter
½ teaspoon seasoned salt
¼ teaspoon garlic powder
¼ teaspoon paprika
¼ teaspoon thyme
   Pepper to taste
¼ cup shredded Cheddar cheese
1 full cup Love

▲ Cut the potato slices with the second-smallest heart cutter (buy a Wilton Heart Cutter). Place on a baking sheet sprayed with nonstick cooking spray.

▲ Combine the butter, seasoned salt, garlic powder, paprika, thyme and pepper in a small bowl. Brush over the potato hearts.

▲ Bake at 400 degrees for 10 to 15 minutes or until the potatoes are tender. Sprinkle with the cheese. Bake for 5 minutes longer.

▲ Add your cup of Love and serve with a warm smile.

Serves 4 to 6

Risotto with Artichokes and Shrimp

Hilda Pope, The Classic Gourmet

6   tablespoons butter
3   shallots or 1 small onion, chopped
2   cups arborio rice
½   cup dry white wine
3   cups chicken stock
3   cups boiling water
8   ounces small shrimp, peeled
2   cups canned artichokes, drained, chopped
     Salt and pepper to taste
     Freshly grated Parmesan cheese to taste

▲ Melt 4 tablespoons of the butter in a heavy saucepan. Sauté the shallots until tender. Add the rice. Sauté until the rice is opaque.

▲ Add the wine. Cook over low heat until completely absorbed.

▲ Heat the chicken stock and boiling water in a small saucepan. Add half the stock to the rice mixture ½ cup at a time, stirring frequently and cooking until the liquid is absorbed after each addition.

▲ Add the shrimp, artichokes, salt and pepper. Add the remaining stock ½ cup at a time and cook until the rice is tender. Stir in the remaining butter and the Parmesan cheese. Serve hot.

Serves 6 to 8

Spinach Grits

Ann Cox, Kroger Food Stores

1   cup quick-cooking grits
4   cups boiling water
½   cup margarine
1   envelope instant onion soup mix
8   ounces shredded sharp Cheddar cheese
2   eggs, beaten
½   cup milk
1   (10-ounce) package frozen chopped spinach, cooked and drained
½   cup shredded sharp Cheddar cheese

▲ Cook the grits in the boiling water in a saucepan using package directions and stirring frequently to avoid sticking and lumps. Stir in the margarine, onion soup mix and 8 ounces cheese. Remove from heat and cool slightly.

▲ Beat in the eggs and milk. Fold in the spinach. Pour into a buttered 9x13-inch baking dish. Top with ½ cup cheese.

▲ Bake at 350 degrees for 45 to 60 minutes or until browned.

Serves 8 to 10

Miss Daisy's Party Squash

Daisy King

1   pound yellow squash, sliced

½   cup mayonnaise

½   cup chopped pecans

¼   cup finely chopped green pepper

1   egg, slightly beaten

½   teaspoon pepper

1   teaspoon salt

1   teaspoon sugar

½   cup minced onion

½   cup shredded sharp Cheddar cheese

¼   cup cracker crumbs

¼   cup butter, sliced

▲ Cook the squash in water to cover in a heavy saucepan until tender. Drain well and mash.

▲ Combine the squash with the mayonnaise, pecans, green pepper, egg, pepper, salt, sugar, onion and cheese in a bowl; mix well. Spoon into a 2-quart baking dish. Top with the cracker crumbs and butter.

▲ Bake at 350 degrees for 35 to 40 minutes or until browned.

Serves 6

Stuffed Yellow Squash

Lynne Tolley, Miss Mary Bobo's Boarding House

3   large yellow squash

4   ounces hot bulk pork sausage

⅓   cup chopped onion

½   cup chopped green bell pepper

½   cup chopped tomato

½   cup grated Parmesan cheese

¾   cup shredded mozzarella cheese

▲ Cut the squash into halves lengthwise. Scoop out the pulp and seeds, leaving 1¼-inch shells; set aside.

▲ Cook the sausage, onion and green pepper in a skillet over medium heat until the sausage is cooked through; drain well. Stir in the tomato and Parmesan cheese.

▲ Spoon the mixture into the squash shells. Place on a baking sheet.

▲ Bake at 350 degrees for 20 minutes. Sprinkle with the mozzarella cheese. Bake for 5 minutes longer or until the cheese is melted.

Serves 2 to 3

Sweet Potato Soufflé

Judy Powell, Holly Berry Inn

3 cups mashed cooked sweet potatoes

1 cup sugar

½ teaspoon salt

2 eggs, slightly beaten

3½ tablespoons melted butter

1 cup milk

1 teaspoon vanilla extract

⅓ cup melted butter

1 cup packed brown sugar

⅓ cup flour

1 cup chopped pecans

1 cup flaked coconut

▲ Beat the sweet potatoes with the sugar in a large bowl. Stir in the salt and eggs. Add 3½ tablespoons butter, milk and vanilla, mixing well. Spoon into a greased baking dish.

▲ Bake at 350 degrees for 35 minutes.

▲ Combine ⅓ cup butter, brown sugar, flour, pecans and coconut in a small bowl, mixing well. Spread over the sweet potatoes.

▲ Bake for 20 minutes longer.

▲ For Sweet Potato Pie, add ¼ cup evaporated milk, ¼ cup sugar, 1 beaten egg, 1 teaspoon each cinnamon and nutmeg and ¼ teaspoon ginger to the sweet potato mixture. Pour into a pie shell and bake as directed until set.

Serves 6

Swiss Vegetable Medley

Lesa Duvall, Potluck Contest Winner

1 (16-ounce) package frozen mixed broccoli, carrots and cauliflower

1 (16-ounce) package frozen mixed broccoli, carrots and water chestnuts

1 (10-ounce) can cream of mushroom soup

1 cup shredded Swiss cheese

½ cup sour cream

¼ teaspoon pepper

1 (2-ounce) jar chopped pimento, drained (optional)

1 (2-ounce) can French-fried onions

▲ Thaw the frozen vegetables. Combine with the soup, ½ cup of the cheese, sour cream, pepper and pimento in a bowl; mix well. Pour into a greased 9x11-inch baking dish.

▲ Bake, covered, at 350 degrees for 30 minutes. Top with the remaining cheese and the French-fried onions.

▲ Bake, uncovered, for 5 minutes longer.

Serves 6

Miss Penny's Sausage Stuffing

Penny Deweese, Miss Penny's

1½ pounds hot Tennessee Pride
    sausage

2   large onions, finely chopped

4   slices bacon

3   cups finely chopped celery

1   (16-ounce) package herb-
    seasoned stuffing mix

4   cups crumbled corn bread

½   cup melted butter

4   eggs, beaten

6   cups hot turkey broth

2   (10-ounce) cans cream of chicken
    soup

▲ Brown the sausage with the onions and bacon in a large skillet over low heat until the sausage is cooked through. Add the celery.

▲ Cook for 5 minutes longer, stirring occasionally; drain.

▲ Combine the stuffing mix, corn bread and butter in a large bowl. Add the eggs and the sausage mixture, mixing well.

▲ Mix the turkey broth with the chicken soup. Pour into the mixture, adding hot water for desired consistency and mixing well. Spoon the mixture into a large baking pan.

▲ Bake at 325 degrees for 15 to 20 minutes.

Makes enough stuffing for a 14- to 20-pound turkey

 Make a delicious Apple Stuffing with equal parts chopped apples and bread cubes. Season with onion, celery, sage and salt.

Tofu Stir-Fry

Slice of Life Restaurant

1   pound tofu, drained, cut into
    cubes
    Tofu Marinade (below)
8   ounces nutritional yeast
¼   cup sesame oil
1   cup chopped onion
1   cup broccoli florets
½   cup chopped celery
1   cup chopped red bell pepper
1   cup sliced mushrooms
½   teaspoon grated fresh gingerroot
1   teaspoon minced garlic
1   tablespoon soy sauce

▲ Marinate the tofu in the Tofu Marinade in a large shallow bowl for 1 to 3 hours, turning occasionally to coat.

▲ Remove the tofu from the marinade and coat with the yeast. Heat the sesame oil in a large skillet. Cook the tofu over medium heat until browned on all sides.

▲ Add the onion, broccoli, celery and red pepper. Stir-fry for 2 to 3 minutes.

▲ Add the mushrooms, garlic and ginger. Stir-fry for 1 minute. Stir in the soy sauce.

▲ Serve over your favorite pasta or rice.

Serves 4

Tofu Marinade

½   cup soy sauce
¼   cup white wine
1   teaspoon chopped garlic
½   cup orange juice
1   tablespoon fennel

▲ Combine the soy sauce, wine, garlic, orange juice and fennel in a large shallow bowl; mix well.

Fried Green Tomatoes Stuffed with Herb Cheese

Daisy King

8 ounces cream cheese, softened

½ cup mixed chopped basil, oregano and thyme

1 teaspoon minced fresh garlic

Salt and pepper to taste

6 green tomatoes, cut into ½-inch slices

3 eggs, beaten

2 cups fine dry bread crumbs

2 tablespoons butter

▲ Mix the cream cheese, basil, oregano, thyme, garlic, salt and pepper in a small bowl. Spread the mixture over half of the tomato slices; top with the remaining slices.

▲ Dip in the eggs; coat with the bread crumbs.

▲ Sauté in the butter in a large skillet until golden brown.

Serves 4 to 6

Stuffed Zucchini

Doc Holliday

4 medium zucchini

½ cup Italian-seasoned bread crumbs

⅓ cup freshly grated Parmesan cheese

1 egg, beaten

½ teaspoon garlic powder

½ teaspoon dried thyme

½ teaspoon dried oregano

½ teaspoon pepper

Salt to taste

¼ cup shredded Cheddar cheese

¼ cup shredded Monterey Jack cheese

▲ Cook the whole zucchini in a large saucepan of boiling water for 15 minutes or until tender. Remove with a slotted spoon; cool slightly.

▲ Combine the bread crumbs, Parmesan cheese, egg, garlic powder, thyme, oregano, pepper and salt in a large bowl; mix well.

▲ Slice the zucchini into halves lengthwise. Scoop out the pulp in the center and drain well, reserving the shells. Stir the pulp into the bread crumb mixture, adding more bread crumbs for desired consistency.

▲ Spoon the mixture into the zucchini shells. Place on a baking sheet. Sprinkle with the Cheddar and Monterey Jack cheeses.

▲ Bake at 350 degrees for 15 minutes or until heated through and bubbly.

Serves 4

Cranberry Pears

Ann Cox, Kroger Food Stores

1 (16-ounce) can whole cranberry sauce
⅓ cup sugar
1 tablespoon fresh lemon juice
¼ teaspoon cinnamon
¼ teaspoon ground ginger
6 fresh pears, peeled, cored and quartered

▲ Combine cranberry sauce, sugar, lemon juice, cinnamon and ginger in a saucepan. Bring to a boil.

▲ Place pear quarters in a 7x11-inch baking dish. Pour cranberry mixture over pears.

▲ Bake, covered, at 350 degrees for 40 minutes or until pears are tender. Serve warm.

Serves 6

Quick Corn Relish

Lynne Tolley, Miss Mary Bobo's Boarding House

1 (12-ounce) can whole kernel corn
½ teaspoon cornstarch
1 small onion, thinly sliced
2 tablespoons chopped green bell pepper
2 tablespoons chopped pimentos
¼ cup vinegar
¼ cup packed light brown sugar
½ teaspoon salt
¼ teaspoon mustard seeds
½ teaspoon celery seeds
¼ teaspoon red pepper sauce

▲ Drain the corn, reserving ¼ cup of the liquid. Set the corn aside. Mix the reserved liquid with the cornstarch in a saucepan. Add the onion, green pepper, pimentos, vinegar, brown sugar, salt, mustard seeds, celery seeds and red pepper sauce.

▲ Bring to a boil; reduce the heat. Simmer for 5 minutes; remove from heat.

▲ Stir in the corn. Let stand to cool. Store in the refrigerator.

Yields 2 cups

Chapter 5
Main Dishes

The NewsChannel 5 team has changed a lot
over the years. Here is a look at the 1968 news team.

NewsChannel5

One of viewers' favorite guests, Miss Lee Reese, generates hundreds of requests for her sewing crafts.

Talk of the Town "Soap Opera Maven" Sharon Frost, answers viewers' questions on the latest daytime dramas.

Picnic Herbed Chicken

John Sarich

½ cup extra-virgin olive oil

2 cloves garlic, mashed

1 chicken, cut into serving pieces

½ teaspoon medium-grind pepper

½ teaspoon salt

2 cups fine dry bread crumbs

2 tablespoons chopped fresh rosemary

2 tablespoons chopped fresh Italian parsley

2 tablespoons chopped fresh oregano

¼ cup grated Parmesan cheese

▲ Combine the olive oil and garlic in a medium bowl. Rinse the chicken and pat dry. Coat with the oil mixture; season with the pepper and salt.

▲ Toss the bread crumbs, rosemary, parsley, oregano and cheese in a small bowl. Coat the chicken with the crumb mixture. Place in a baking dish.

▲ Bake at 325 degrees for 40 minutes, turning once.

Serves 4

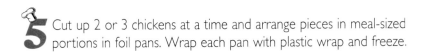 Cut up 2 or 3 chickens at a time and arrange pieces in meal-sized portions in foil pans. Wrap each pan with plastic wrap and freeze.

Roast Chicken with Herbs and White Wine

Florine Johns, Nashville Herb Society

1   (3- to 3½-pound) whole chicken
¾   cup dry white wine
    Olive oil
1   teaspoon dried oregano
1   teaspoon ground cumin
    Bouquet garni of fresh rosemary, sage and thyme
3   to 4 whole cloves garlic
    Garlic powder and paprika to taste
2   to 4 cloves garlic, sliced

▲ Rinse the chicken and pat dry. Remove excess fat. Place breast side down in a shallow nonreactive roasting pan. Pour the wine over the chicken. Marinate in the refrigerator for 1 to 2 hours.

▲ Remove the chicken from the marinade; pat dry. Place breast side up on an oiled rack in the roasting pan, leaving the wine in the pan. Rub the chicken with olive oil.

▲ Sprinkle the cavity with ½ teaspoon oregano and ½ teaspoon cumin. Add the bouquet garni and the whole garlic cloves.

▲ Sprinkle the outside of the chicken with the remaining oregano, cumin, garlic powder and paprika. Tuck the sliced garlic between the wings and thighs.

▲ Place the chicken in a preheated 450-degree oven; reduce the oven temperature to 350 degrees.

▲ Bake for 30 minutes. Cover the breast portion with a loose tent of parchment paper or foil. Bake for 30 to 40 minutes longer (20 minutes per pound) or until cooked through, basting frequently with the pan drippings. May add additional wine or water to the pan drippings if needed.

Serves 4 to 6

Swett's Famous Southern Fried Chicken

David Swett, Swett's Restaurant

1   (3-pound) chicken
1   egg
½   cup water
2   teaspoons salt
2   teaspoons cracked pepper
2   teaspoons granulated garlic
4   cups flour
    Vegetable oil for frying

▲ Rinse the chicken and pat dry. Cut into 8 serving pieces; set aside.

▲ Beat the egg and water with 1 teaspoon salt, 1 teaspoon pepper and 1 teaspoon garlic in a bowl.

▲ Combine the flour with the remaining salt, pepper and garlic in a large bowl.

▲ Dip the chicken in the egg mixture. Coat twice in the seasoned flour.

▲ Heat the oil to 325 degrees in a deep fryer. Add the chicken.

▲ Fry until golden brown and the temperature on a meat thermometer registers 180 degrees when inserted in chicken.

Serves 4

For Crispy Fried Chicken, substitute cornstarch for half the flour and add ½ teaspoon baking powder. Season as usual.

Chicken with Brie and Apples

Jody Faison, Faison's Restaurant

1 skinless boneless chicken breast
1 tablespoon chopped green onions
1 tablespoon minced garlic
¼ cup chopped cashews
2 tablespoons melted margarine
1 Red Delicious apple, cut into wedges
¼ cup heavy cream
5 ounces Brie cheese
Juice of ½ lemon
Fresh tarragon to taste
Salt, pepper and granulated garlic to taste

▲ Rinse the chicken and pat dry. Sauté the green onions, garlic and cashews in the margarine in a skillet for 1 minute. Add the chicken and apple.

▲ Cook for 3 minutes, turning once. Add the cream and Brie.

▲ Cook for 2 minutes longer or until the cheese is melted.

▲ Stir in the lemon juice, tarragon, salt, pepper and garlic. Serve immediately.

Serves 1

Chipotle Chicken with Mango and Cranberries

Al Anderson, Jr., Santa Fe Restaurant and Cantina

4   (8-ounce) chicken breasts
    Vegetable oil for sautéing plus 1
    teaspoon vegetable oil
¼   cup packed dark brown sugar
¼   teaspoon freshly ground cloves
2   tablespoons ground ginger
⅛   teaspoon minced jalapeño
½   teaspoon minced chipotle in
    Poblo sauce
½   teaspoon soy sauce (optional)
½   cup fresh cranberries
¼   cup fresh orange juice
½   cup peeled, chopped mangoes,
    chilled

▲ Rinse the chicken and pat dry. Sauté in a small amount of vegetable oil in a large skillet until browned on both sides. Remove from the skillet and keep warm.

▲ Add 1 teaspoon oil, brown sugar, cloves, ginger, jalapeño, chipotle, soy sauce, cranberries and orange juice to the skillet.

▲ Cook over medium heat until the sauce begins to thicken and bubble, stirring frequently. Add the chicken and mangoes to the mixture.

▲ Cook until heated through, coating the chicken with the sauce. Serve with rice.

Serves 4

Mother and Child Chicken

Yoko Watanabe, Potluck Contest Winner

½ cup soy sauce

½ cup sugar

1½ cups water

1 pound skinless boneless chicken breasts

½ onion, sliced

8 mushrooms, sliced

12 snow peas, blanched

8 eggs, beaten

8 cups hot cooked rice

▲ Combine the soy sauce, sugar and water in a large skillet. Bring to a boil; remove from the heat.

▲ Rinse the chicken and pat dry. Cut into cubes. Add the chicken, onion and mushrooms to the sauce.

▲ Cook over medium heat until the chicken is cooked through. Add the snow peas and eggs.

▲ Cook, covered, for 20 seconds.

▲ Spoon over the rice in individual serving bowls.

Serves 8

5 For Grilled Ginger Chicken, marinate chicken breast fillets in a mixture of ½ cup soy sauce, minced garlic, ¾ teaspoon ginger, 2 tablespoons sugar and 1 ounce sherry for 4 to 6 hours. Grill for 15 minutes or until cooked through.

TASTE OF **5** THE TOWN

New Orleans-Style Chicken

Randy Rayburn, Sunset Grill

1   tablespoon paprika
1   tablespoon dried basil
2   teaspoons salt
2   teaspoons onion powder
2   teaspoons dried oregano
1   teaspoon minced garlic
1   teaspoon white pepper
1   teaspoon dry mustard
½   teaspoon black pepper
½   teaspoon coriander
¾   teaspoon dried thyme
4   (8-ounce) skinless chicken breasts
4   cups chopped onion
2   cups chopped green bell pepper
2   cups sliced mushrooms
3   bay leaves
2½ cups chicken stock
¼   cup flour
3   cups torn fresh spinach
2   large tomatoes, chopped

▲ Combine the paprika, basil, salt, onion powder, oregano, garlic, white pepper, dry mustard, black pepper, coriander and thyme in a large bowl; mix well.

▲ Rinse the chicken and pat dry. Sprinkle with 5 teaspoons of the spice mixture, rubbing well. Reserve the remaining spice mixture.

▲ Heat a nonstick 5-quart saucepan over high heat for 4 minutes. Add the chicken.

▲ Cook for 10 minutes or until browned on each side. Remove the chicken and keep warm. Add the onion, green pepper, mushrooms, bay leaves and reserved spice mixture.

▲ Sauté the vegetables for 5 minutes or until browned, scraping the pan frequently. Add ½ cup of the chicken stock.

▲ Cook for 4 minutes or until the liquid is absorbed. Add the flour.

▲ Cook for 2 minutes or until browned, stirring constantly. Add the spinach, tomatoes and remaining chicken stock.

▲ Bring to a boil. Add the chicken. Reduce the heat to low.

▲ Simmer for 20 minutes. Serve over rice.

Serves 4

Sautéed Chicken with Mediterranean Vegetables

David Swett, Swett's Restaurant

4 to 6 ounces boneless skinless chicken breast

Salt, white pepper, Hungarian paprika and jerk seasoning to taste

Olive oil for sautéing

3 ounces zucchini, sliced

3 ounces summer squash, sliced

2 ounces tomatoes, chopped

2 ounces onion, sliced

2 ounces green bell pepper, chopped

2 tablespoons chopped fresh basil

2 tablespoons chopped fresh thyme

2 tablespoons chopped fresh rosemary

2 tablespoons chopped fresh oregano

2 tablespoons minced garlic

¼ cup chicken broth

▲ Rinse the chicken and pat dry. Season with salt, white pepper, paprika and jerk seasoning.

▲ Sauté in a small amount of olive oil in a large deep skillet until browned on both sides; remove the chicken and keep warm.

▲ Add the zucchini, summer squash, tomatoes, onion, bell pepper, basil, thyme, rosemary, oregano and garlic to the skillet. Add a small amount of olive oil if needed.

▲ Cook over high heat until the vegetables are tender, stirring occasionally. Pour in the chicken broth.

▲ Simmer until heated through. Spoon the vegetable mixture onto a serving plate; top with the chicken.

Serves 1

TASTE OF **5** THE TOWN

Steak and Chicken Fajitas

Ross El-Bobou, Safari Restaurant

1   cup soy sauce

2   cups pineapple juice

2   tablespoons minced garlic

1   tablespoon ground ginger

1   cup honey

1   cup lime juice

8   ounces boneless skinless chicken breast

8   ounces flank steak

1   green bell pepper, julienned

1   red bell pepper, julienned

1   yellow onion, sliced

8   (6-inch) flour tortillas

Shredded lettuce

Sour cream

Shredded Cheddar cheese and Monterey Jack cheese

▲ Combine the soy sauce, pineapple juice, garlic, ginger, honey and lime juice in a bowl; mix well.

▲ Rinse the chicken and pat dry. Pour ¾ of the mixture over the steak and chicken in a shallow bowl, turning to coat. Marinate in the refrigerator for 12 hours. Drain and discard the marinade.

▲ Pour the remaining marinade mixture over the bell peppers and onion in a small shallow bowl. Marinate for 2 hours. Drain, reserving the marinade.

▲ Grill the steak and chicken over hot coals until cooked through. Cool slightly; cut into strips.

▲ Heat a cast-iron skillet to 200 degrees; remove from the heat. Place the bell peppers and onion in the skillet immediately. Top with the steak and chicken. Pour in the reserved marinade.

▲ Place the tortillas on individual serving plates. Spoon the chicken and vegetable mixture evenly onto the tortillas. Top with lettuce, sour cream and cheeses. Roll up and serve immediately.

Serves 8

Spicy Ginger Chicken

*A Friend of **Talk of the Town***

2 tablespoons soy sauce

2 tablespoons fish sauce

2 tablespoons whiskey

½ teaspoon hot chili paste

2 tablespoons tapioca starch

¼ teaspoon sugar

1 teaspoon vinegar

8 ounces skinless boneless chicken breast

1 egg white

4 tablespoons peanut oil

2 tablespoons minced shallots

1 teaspoon minced garlic

1 teaspoon minced gingerroot

1 red bell pepper, sliced

1 green bell pepper, sliced

1 (8-ounce) can bamboo shoots, drained

1 teaspoon sesame oil

▲ Combine the soy sauce, fish sauce, whiskey, chili paste, 1 tablespoon of the tapioca starch, sugar and vinegar in a bowl. Mix well and set aside.

▲ Rinse the chicken and pat dry. Cut into small strips. Beat the egg white with the remaining tapioca starch in a small bowl. Add the chicken strips, tossing to coat.

▲ Heat 3 tablespoons of the peanut oil in a wok over high heat. Stir-fry the chicken for 1 minute. Remove and set aside.

▲ Heat the remaining peanut oil in the wok. Stir-fry the shallots, garlic and ginger for 1 minute. Add the bell peppers and bamboo shoots.

▲ Stir-fry over high heat for 1 to 2 minutes. Add the chicken and the soy sauce mixture.

▲ Cook until the sauce is thickened and the chicken is cooked through, stirring frequently. Add the sesame oil, tossing to mix. Serve with cooked rice.

Serves 2

Puffy Chicken Chiles Rellenos

Ann Cox, Kroger Food Stores

1½ cups chopped cooked chicken

3 (4-ounce) cans chopped green chiles, drained

4 flour tortillas, cut into halves

16 ounces Monterey Jack cheese, shredded

2 to 3 Roma tomatoes, seeded, chopped

8 eggs, lightly beaten

½ cup milk

2 tablespoons flour

½ teaspoon salt

½ teaspoon pepper

½ teaspoon cumin

½ teaspoon garlic powder

½ teaspoon onion salt

Paprika to taste

½ cup sour cream (optional)

¼ cup chopped green onions (optional)

▲ Layer half the chicken, half the green chiles, half the tortillas and half the cheese in a 2½-quart baking dish. Top with the tomatoes. Repeat the layers with the remaining chicken, green chiles, tortillas and cheese. Beat the eggs, milk, flour, salt, pepper, cumin, garlic powder and onion salt in a bowl. Pour over the layers. Sprinkle with paprika.

▲ Bake at 350 degrees for 35 to 40 minutes or until golden and puffy. Cool for 10 to 15 minutes before serving. Top with sour cream and green onions.

Serves 6 to 8

Minnie Pearl's Chicken Tetrazzini

Daisy King, **Miss Daisy Celebrates Tennessee**

2   cups chopped celery

1½ cups chopped onion

3   tablespoons butter or margarine

2   cups chicken broth

1   tablespoon Worcestershire sauce
    Salt and pepper to taste

1   (10-ounce) can cream of
    mushroom soup

½   cup milk

1   cup shredded sharp Cheddar
    cheese

8   ounces spaghetti, cooked, drained

6   cups chopped cooked chicken

½   cup sliced pimento-stuffed olives

1   cup chopped pecans

▲ Sauté the celery and onion in the butter in a large saucepan until the vegetables are tender. Add the chicken broth, Worcestershire sauce, salt and pepper.

▲ Simmer for 15 minutes, stirring occasionally. Add the soup, milk and cheese; mix well.

▲ Remove from the heat. Add the spaghetti. Let stand for 1 hour.

▲ Stir the chicken and olives into the spaghetti mixture. Spoon into a greased 9x13-inch baking dish. Top with the pecans.

▲ Bake at 350 degrees for 20 to 25 minutes or until hot and bubbly.

Serves 12

Turkey Tortilla Casserole

Betty Rohde, **Sofat, Lowfat, Nofat Cookbook**

2 pounds ground turkey

1 clove garlic minced

1 cup chopped onion

1 (15-ounce) can tomato sauce

1 envelope taco seasoning mix

1 (4-ounce) can chopped green chiles, drained

1 teaspoon chili powder, or to taste

Salt and pepper to taste

12 (6-inch) corn tortillas

1 (10-ounce) can low-fat cream of chicken soup

¾ cup skim milk

2 cups shredded fat-free Cheddar cheese

▲ Brown the turkey, garlic and onion in a large skillet over medium heat, stirring frequently. Drain in a colander and rinse with hot water to remove fat; drain again.

▲ Wipe the skillet with a paper towel to remove fat. Add the turkey mixture to the skillet. Add the tomato sauce, taco mix, green chiles, chili powder, salt and pepper, mixing well. Simmer until heated through.

▲ Line a 9x13-inch baking dish with half of the tortillas. Top with the turkey mixture. Arrange the remaining tortillas over the turkey. Spread the soup over the tortillas. Pour the milk over the soup. Sprinkle with the cheese.

▲ Bake at 350 degrees for 45 minutes. Serve with salsa and fat-free sour cream.

Serves 6

Beef with Oyster Sauce

Sandy Wolchok

½ teaspoon baking soda
1 teaspoon sugar
1 tablespoon cornstarch
1 tablespoon soy sauce
3 tablespoons water
1 pound flank steak
2 tablespoons oyster sauce
1 tablespoon water
1 teaspoon sugar
½ teaspoon cornstarch
½ teaspoon sesame oil
8 ounces broccoli
¾ cup vegetable oil
½ tablespoon dry sherry
1 teaspoon sugar
15 (1-inch) green onion pieces
15 slices gingerroot

▲ Combine ½ teaspoon baking soda, 1 teaspoon sugar, 1 tablespoon cornstarch, soy sauce and 3 tablespoons water in a shallow bowl; mix well.

▲ Cut the flank steak into thin 1-inch squares. Add to the marinade. Marinate for 30 minutes or longer.

▲ Mix the oyster sauce, 1 tablespoon water, 1 teaspoon sugar, ½ teaspoon cornstarch and sesame oil in a bowl; set aside.

▲ Cut the broccoli into bite-sized pieces. Boil or microwave in a small amount of water in a saucepan until tender-crisp.

▲ Heat 2 tablespoons of the vegetable oil in a wok or skillet. Stir in the sherry and 1 teaspoon sugar. Stir-fry the broccoli in the mixture for 1 to 2 minutes. Remove and set aside.

▲ Heat ½ cup of the vegetable oil in the wok to 300 degrees. Add the flank steak. Stir-fry until medium-rare. Remove and set aside.

▲ Heat the remaining vegetable oil in the wok. Stir-fry the green onion pieces and ginger for 30 seconds.

▲ Add the flank steak. Cook over high heat for 30 to 60 seconds. Add the broccoli and the oyster sauce mixture.

▲ Cook until the sauce is thickened and heated through. Serve with cooked rice.

Serves 2 to 4

TASTE OF **5** THE TOWN

Crescent-Topped Beef Potpie

Tammy Algood, Tennessee Agricultural Extension Service

1   boneless top sirloin steak

¼   teaspoon pepper

1   (16-ounce) package mixed frozen green beans, broccoli, onion and red pepper

2   tablespoons water

½   teaspoon dried thyme

1   (12-ounce) jar mushroom gravy

1   (8-count) can refrigerated crescent rolls

▲ Trim all fat from the steak. Slice lengthwise into strips; cut crosswise into ½-inch-thick slices.

▲ Spray a large skillet with nonstick cooking spray. Heat over medium-high heat until very hot.

▲ Stir-fry the steak in the hot skillet ½ at a time for 1 minute. Remove from the skillet and season with pepper.

▲ Add the mixed vegetables to the skillet. Stir in the water and thyme.

▲ Cook for 3 minutes or until the vegetables are thawed, stirring frequently. Add the mushroom gravy.

▲ Bring the mixture to a boil; remove from the heat. Stir in the steak. Spoon the mixture into a baking dish.

▲ Separate the crescent roll dough into 8 triangles. Roll up halfway, beginning from the widest end. Arrange over the steak mixture with the pointed ends toward the center.

▲ Bake at 375 degrees for 17 to 19 minutes or until the rolls are golden brown.

Serves 4

Yakiniku Donburi (Fried Beef and Vegetables on Rice)

Yoko Watanabe, Potluck Contest Winner

¼ cup ground ginger

¼ cup toasted sesame seeds

½ cup soy sauce

¼ cup sugar

2 tablespoons sake or mirin

2 tablespoons sesame oil

2 pounds sirloin steak or lean beef
    Vegetable oil for frying

1 cup onion, cut into ¼-inch strips

½ red bell pepper, cut into ¼-inch strips

½ yellow bell pepper, cut into ¼-inch strips

½ green bell pepper, cut into ¼-inch strips

8 cups hot cooked rice

▲ Combine the ginger, sesame seeds, soy sauce, sugar, sake and sesame oil in a shallow bowl; mix well.

▲ Cut the steak into ¼-inch strips. Place in the soy sauce marinade. Marinate in the refrigerator for 1 hour. Remove the steak, reserving the marinade.

▲ Heat a small amount of oil in a large skillet until very hot. Add the onion and bell peppers.

▲ Stir-fry until tender-crisp. Remove and keep warm.

▲ Stir-fry the beef in the skillet over high heat until cooked through. Add the vegetables and the reserved marinade.

▲ Cook until heated through. Serve over rice in individual bowls.

Serves 4

Hungarian Goulash

Helma Ritter, Ole Heidelberg Restaurant

1	pound lean beef, cut into cubes
1	pound pork, cut into cubes
3	large onions, sliced
1	clove garlic, minced
	Shortening for sautéing
	Pinch of caraway seeds
	Salt and pepper to taste
2	to 3 tablespoons Hungarian paprika
1	cup chopped tomatoes
1	egg
½	cup flour

▲ Sauté the beef, pork, onions and garlic in the shortening in a large skillet until the meat is cooked through.

▲ Add the caraway seeds, salt, pepper, paprika and tomatoes.

▲ Simmer until the mixture thickens slightly, stirring frequently.

▲ Mix the egg and flour in a bowl. Add enough water to make a soft dough.

▲ Drop the mixture by tablespoonfuls into boiling water in a saucepan.

▲ Cook until the dumplings float to the top. Drain well.

▲ Serve the goulash mixture over the dumplings.

Serves 4 to 6

5 Hungarian paprika is considered to be a superior variety of paprika. This full-flavored variety comes in both mild and hot forms. It should be stored in a cool, dark place for no more than 6 months.

Tennessee Tenderloin Tips

Lynne Tolley, Miss Mary Bobo's Boarding House

2 pounds beef tenderloin tips, thinly sliced
¼ cup butter
2 teaspoons salt
1 cup sliced mushrooms
¼ cup chopped onion
1 clove garlic, minced
½ cup burgundy
½ cup Jack Daniel's Whiskey
1 cup crushed tomatoes
2 teaspoons sugar

▲ Sauté the beef in the butter in a skillet a small amount at a time until browned.

▲ Add the salt, mushrooms, onion and garlic.

▲ Simmer for 3 to 5 minutes, adding more butter if needed.

▲ Stir in the wine, whiskey, tomatoes and sugar.

▲ Simmer for 30 minutes or until the beef is tender. Serve with mashed potatoes or rice.

Serves 4

 When purchasing beef, choose brightly colored, red to deep red cuts. Marbeling should be moderate.

Twenty-Minute Tamale Pie

Doc Holliday

2   tablespoons butter

1   pound lean ground beef

1   onion, chopped

1   (17-ounce) can whole kernel corn

1   (16-ounce) can stewed tomatoes, drained

1   cup sour cream

1   cup yellow cornmeal

1   (4-ounce) can sliced black olives, drained

1   tablespoon chili powder

1   teaspoon salt

½   teaspoon cumin

2   cups shredded Monterey Jack cheese

▲ Melt the butter in a large skillet over medium-high heat. Add the ground beef and onion.

▲ Cook for 5 minutes or until the beef is lightly browned, stirring occasionally; drain well.

▲ Stir in the undrained corn, tomatoes, sour cream, cornmeal, olives, chili powder, salt and cumin.

▲ Spoon into a lightly greased 9x13-inch baking dish. Sprinkle with the cheese. Cover with foil.

▲ Bake at 375 degrees for 20 minutes. May uncover during the last 5 minutes to brown on top. Serve hot with salsa.

Serves 6 to 8

Beef and Sausage Shish Kabobs

Doc Holliday

4   hot Italian sausages, cut into 1-inch slices

2   tablespoons peanut oil

3   tablespoons dry sherry

3   tablespoons soy sauce

2   green onions, finely chopped

1   tablespoon brown sugar

1   teaspoon Grey Poupon mustard

8   ounces boneless top round, cut into 1½-inch cubes

8   ounces mushrooms

1   green bell pepper, cut into 1½-inch pieces

1   large onion, cut into 1½-inch pieces

1   large zucchini, cut into ½-inch slices

6   Roma tomatoes, cut into halves

▲ Cook the sausage in a large heavy skillet over medium heat for 8 minutes or until cooked through, stirring occasionally; drain well.

▲ Combine the peanut oil, sherry, soy sauce, green onions, brown sugar and mustard in a large bowl; mix well. Add the sausage, beef, mushrooms, green pepper, onion and zucchini, tossing to coat. Marinate, covered, in the refrigerator for 8 hours to overnight, stirring occasionally.

▲ Preheat the grill or broiler. Arrange the vegetables and meat alternately on metal skewers or bamboo skewers soaked in water, beginning and ending with a tomato half.

▲ Grill or broil for 10 minutes or until the beef is cooked through and the vegetables are browned, turning occasionally. Serve immediately.

Serves 6

When grilling food on a skewer, position the pieces of food about ¼ inch apart to insure even cooking.

Upside-Down Pizza

*A Friend of **Talk of the Town***

1   pound ground beef
1   onion, chopped
½   tablespoon chopped parsley
1   envelope spaghetti sauce mix
1   (15-ounce) can tomato sauce
2   cups shredded mozzarella cheese
2   eggs
1   cup milk
1   tablespoon vegetable oil
1   cup flour
¼   teaspoon salt
½   cup grated Parmesan cheese
    Paprika to taste

▲ Combine the ground beef and onion in a microwave-safe bowl. Microwave, covered, on High for 9 minutes, stirring every 3 minutes. Stir in the parsley, spaghetti sauce mix and tomato sauce.

▲ Microwave, covered, for 3 minutes. Spoon the mixture into a greased 9x13-inch baking dish. Top with the mozzarella cheese.

▲ Beat the eggs, milk and oil in a small bowl until foamy. Add the flour and salt, beating until smooth. Pour over the cheese in the baking dish, spreading evenly. Top with the Parmesan cheese and paprika.

▲ Bake at 400 degrees for 30 minutes or until golden brown. Cut into squares to serve.

Serves 8

Boneless Leg of Lamb

Penny Deweese, Miss Penny's

1   boneless leg of lamb, rolled and tied
3   teaspoons garlic powder
    Salt and pepper to taste
¼   cup rosemary
1   tablespoon seasoned salt

▲ Place the lamb fat side up on a rack in a shallow roasting pan. Rub with a mixture of the garlic powder, salt, pepper, rosemary and seasoned salt.

▲ Bake at 325 degrees for 2¼ hours or until a meat thermometer registers 160 degrees.

▲ Remove to a serving platter. Let stand for 10 minutes before carving. Serve with pepper jelly.

Serves 4 to 6

Roasted Rack of Lamb with Pepper Jelly and Mashed Potatoes

Émile Labrousse, Arthur's Restaurant

Pepper Jelly

1	red bell pepper, sliced
1	green bell pepper, sliced
1	yellow bell pepper, sliced
1½	pounds sugar
1	cup red wine vinegar
2	tablespoons olive oil
4	jalapeños, finely chopped

▲ Purée the bell peppers in a food processor. Combine with the sugar, vinegar and oil in a small saucepan.

▲ Bring to a boil; reduce heat. Simmer for 3 minutes or until the jelly is thickened, skimming off the foam with a ladle.

▲ Remove from the heat. Stir in the jalapeños. Cover and keep warm at room temperature.

Rack of Lamb

3	racks of lamb
2	tablespoons olive oil
	Salt and pepper to taste

▲ Preheat the oven to 425 degrees. Brush the lamb with olive oil; season with salt and pepper. Place on a rack in a shallow pan.

▲ Roast for 20 minutes. Remove from oven and keep warm.

Mashed Potatoes

6	medium potatoes, peeled, cubed
	Salt to taste
1½	cups buttermilk
	Pepper to taste

▲ Cook the potatoes in salted water in a saucepan until tender; drain. Stir in the buttermilk. Mash the potatoes until smooth. Season with salt and pepper.

▲ To serve, spoon the potatoes into the center of 6 serving plates. Spoon some of the pepper jelly around the potatoes.

▲ Carve the racks of lamb and arrange over the potatoes. Drizzle with more pepper jelly. Serve immediately, garnished with asparagus.

Serves 6

Mid-Eastern Skillet Dinner

Marie Rama, "The Lemon Lady"

8   ounces ground lamb

8   ounces ground turkey

1   teaspoon garlic powder

1   teaspoon crushed Italian
    seasoning, or ½ teaspoon each
    crushed dried oregano and basil

2   cups cooked garbanzo beans or
    cooked white beans

2   medium tomatoes, chopped
    Juice of 1 lemon

2   tablespoons tomato paste

¼   cup water

2   teaspoons sugar

1   teaspoon crushed dried mint
    leaves
    Grated peel of ½ lemon

▲ Mix the lamb, turkey, garlic powder and Italian seasoning in a large bowl. Shape into 8 small patties.

▲ Brown the patties in a large greased skillet over medium-high heat for 10 to 12 minutes; drain well

▲ Add the garbanzo beans, tomatoes, lemon juice, tomato paste, water, sugar and mint leaves.

▲ Bring to a boil; reduce heat to low. Cook, covered, for 20 minutes, stirring occasionally. Uncover and cook for 5 minutes longer or until the sauce is slightly thickened. Stir in the lemon peel.

Serves 4

5 Store ground lamb and small cuts of lamb, loosely wrapped in waxed paper, in the coldest part of the refrigerator for up to 3 days. Larger cuts like roast may be stored for up to 5 days.

TASTE OF **5** THE TOWN

Country Ham

Flaudine Adams, The Shaker Tavern, South Union, Kentucky

1 country ham
½ pound brown sugar
1 quart vinegar
Whole cloves
Orange slices
1 cup bourbon

▲ Select a country ham aged 6 months to no more than 1 year. Your grocer can tell you the age. Have the "hock" removed when you purchase the ham, or you can remove it with a hacksaw.

▲ Soak the ham in water for 24 to 48 hours. Combine 1 pound brown sugar with a quart of vinegar in a cooking pot large enough to hold the entire ham. Stir the mixture until the sugar is dissolved. Add the ham fat side up and enough hot water to cover.

▲ Simmer over very low heat for 20 minutes per pound but do not allow the liquid to boil.

▲ Remove the ham from the heat and let stand to cool. Remove the ham carefully to a platter. Trim the fat to ¼ inch. Stud the ham with whole cloves and orange slices.

▲ Place in a large pan lined with heavy-duty foil. Pour 1 cup bourbon over the ham. Cover with foil, sealing the edges.

▲ Bake at 350 degrees for 1 hour. Remove the foil. Bake for 30 minutes longer to brown the outside. Let stand to cool. Chill in the refrigerator for 8 hours to overnight before slicing into thin slices.

 Never discard the ham bone. Freeze it for later use to flavor soups, stews, beans or broth.

Roast Pork with Basil and Mushroom Stuffing

Judy Powell, Holly Berry Inn

1   pound mushrooms
1   cup chopped basil leaves
½   cup chopped onion
1   teaspoon salt
½   teaspoon pepper
1   (4- to 5-pound) pork loin roast
     Salt to taste
1   (17-ounce) can chicken broth
2   tablespoons butter
¼   cup flour

▲ Reserve a few of the best mushrooms for garnish. Trim and flute the tops. Trim and clip the remaining mushrooms.

▲ Reserve 2 tablespoons of the basil. Combine the remaining basil, mushrooms, onion, 1 teaspoon salt and pepper in a bowl, mixing gently.

▲ Place the pork roast on a flat surface. Cut the pork roast almost into halves, but do not cut through. Spread the roast open. Spoon the mushroom mixture over the roast. Roll up to enclose the filling, and tie with a string every 3 inches to secure.

▲ Place the roast on a rack in a roasting pan. Sprinkle with salt. Pour ¼ cup of the chicken broth around the roast.

▲ Roast at 325 degrees for 2½ hours or until a meat thermometer inserted in the center of roast registers 170 degrees. Remove the roast to a platter and keep warm. Reserve the pan drippings.

▲ Reserve ½ cup of the remaining chicken broth. Pour the remaining chicken broth into a sauté pan. Bring to a boil. Add the reserved pan drippings and butter.

▲ Bring the mixture to a boil. Stir the flour into the reserved chicken broth. Add to the pan.

▲ Cook until the mixture is thickened, stirring frequently. Stir in the reserved basil.

▲ Garnish the roast with the reserved mushrooms. Serve the sauce on the side with the roast.

Serves 6 to 8

Smoked Pork Loin Medallions with Maple Walnut Butter

*A Friend of **Talk of the Town***

Maple Walnut Butter

1   pint heavy cream
1   pound butter, softened
½   cup roasted walnuts
½   cup maple syrup
1   teaspoon nutmeg
2   teaspoons cinnamon
¼   cup apple juice
    Salt and pepper to taste

▲ Bring the cream to a boil in a heavy saucepan. Cook until reduced by half; remove from the heat.

▲ Add the butter, whipping until it has completely melted. Add the walnuts, maple syrup, nutmeg, cinnamon and apple juice, stirring well. Season with salt and pepper.

Smoked Pork Loin

4   cups hickory chips
1   whole pork loin
¼   cup kosher salt
½   cup lemon pepper

▲ Soak hickory chips in water in a pan for 24 hours.

▲ Coat the pork loin with the salt and lemon pepper. Place in a perforated 4-inch hotel pan.

▲ Place a solid 4-inch hotel pan over 2 burners on the stove. Fill with 2 piles of the soaked hickory chips. Arrange the perforated pan inside the solid pan. Cover securely with heavy foil. Make 2 to 3 slits in the foil.

▲ Turn both burners to high. Smoke the pork for 15 minutes. Transfer the pans to the oven.

▲ Bake at 350 degrees for 15 minutes or until cooked through. Let cool slightly. Slice the pork loin into 1-inch-thick rounds.

▲ Arrange on serving plates and top with the maple walnut butter.

Serves 6 to 8

Sauerkraut Casserole

Ruth Morgan, Potluck Contest Winner

1   pound mild Italian sausage links, cut into 1-inch slices

1   large onion, chopped

2   apples, peeled, quartered

1   (27-ounce) can sauerkraut

1   cup water

½   cup packed brown sugar

2   teaspoons caraway seeds

▲ Brown the sausage and onion in a large skillet until the sausage is cooked through; drain well. Stir in the apples, undrained sauerkraut, water, brown sugar and caraway seeds. Spoon into a 2½-quart baking dish.

▲ Bake, covered, at 350 degrees for 1 hour. Serve garnished with parsley.

Serves 6 to 8

Sausage, Potatoes and Leeks

Doc Holliday

4   teaspoons Grey Poupon Spicy Brown mustard

¼   cup red wine vinegar

2   garlic cloves, pressed

½   cup olive oil

    Salt and freshly ground pepper to taste

4   large leeks

4   cups chicken stock

12 medium new potatoes

1   pound smoked kielbasa sausage, cut ⅛ inch thick

▲ Whisk the mustard, vinegar and garlic in a small bowl. Add the oil slowly, whisking constantly until thickened. Season with salt and pepper; set aside.

▲ Slice the pale green part of the leeks into thin rounds; reserve. Chop coarsely the white parts. Combine with the chicken stock in a saucepan.

▲ Boil for 30 minutes or until the stock is reduced to 1¼ cups. Strain through a sieve into a large saucepan, pressing on the leeks with a spoon; discard the cooked leeks. Set the stock aside.

▲ Place the potatoes in enough salted water to cover. Bring to a boil; reduce the heat. Simmer for 30 minutes or until the potatoes are tender. Drain and cool slightly. Peel and cut into ¼-inch rounds. Transfer to a large bowl.

▲ Bring the reduced stock to a boil; reduce the heat to medium. Add the reserved leeks and the sausage. Cook for 5 minutes; drain, reserving the stock.

▲ Pour 1 cup of the reserved stock over the potatoes, tossing gently. Add the leeks and sausage. Remove the garlic from the mustard mixture. Add the mustard mixture to the potatoes, tossing to coat. Season to taste.

Serves 8

Indian Sugar Pumpkins

Dave Mason

1　(4- to 5-pound) pumpkin
¼　cup honey
¼　cup packed brown sugar
1　tablespoon rubbed sage
　　Salt and white pepper to taste
3　pounds venison, beef, turkey or
　　vegetables
¼　cup chopped green onions
3　cups long grain wild rice

▲ Cut off the top of the pumpkin and reserve. Scoop out and discard the seeds and pulp, leaving a 1-inch shell. Spread the honey, brown sugar, sage, salt and white pepper evenly over the inside of the pumpkin; set aside.

▲ Brown the venison and green onions in a small amount of oil in a large skillet; drain.

▲ Cook the rice using package directions. Stir into the venison mixture. Spoon into the prepared pumpkin. Cover with the reserved top of the pumpkin. Place in a pan filled with 1 inch of water.

▲ Bake at 375 degrees for 1 hour, adding additional water if necessary.

Serves 6 to 8

Sure-Shot Rabbit

Fate Thomas

2　cups white vinegar
2　bay leaves
1　medium onion, chopped
1　rabbit, dressed
1　to 2 quarts water
1　tablespoon garlic powder
1　teaspoon seasoned salt
½　teaspoon meat tenderizer
1　cup red cooking wine
　　Barbecue sauce

▲ Combine the vinegar, bay leaves and onion in a large shallow dish. Add the rabbit. Marinate for 8 hours to overnight. Drain, discarding the marinade.

▲ Place the rabbit in a large stockpot with 1 to 2 quarts of water, garlic powder, seasoned salt, meat tenderizer and wine.

▲ Bring to a boil. Cook for 2 hours over high heat, adding additional water if necessary; drain. Remove the rabbit to a rack in a roasting pan.

▲ Bake at 375 to 300 degrees for 3½ to 4 hours or until tender, basting frequently with the barbecue sauce.

Serves 2

Venison Chops, Country Ham and Wild Mushroom Sauce

Craig Jervis, The Mad Platter

Marinated Venison Chops

1   cup red wine
1   cup olive oil
     Julienned onions
     Crushed garlic
     Cracked black pepper
     Freshly chopped rosemary
4   venison chops
8   slices country ham, presoaked in
     water

▲ Combine the wine, oil, onions, garlic, black pepper and rosemary in a large shallow dish, mixing well. Add the venison chops. Marinate in the refrigerator for 3 to 12 hours, turning occasionally. Drain and discard the marinade.

▲ Heat a large skillet sprayed with nonstick cooking spray over high heat. Add the chops. Sear the chops on both sides; reduce the heat. Add the country ham.

▲ Cook over medium-low heat until the ham is of desired doneness.

▲ Arrange the ham on warmed serving plates. Top with the venison chops. Cover with the Wild Mushroom Sauce and serve immediately.

Wild Mushroom Sauce

1   teaspoon finely chopped shallots
1   teaspoon butter
½   cup red wine
2   cups quartered chanterelle
     mushrooms
1   cup prepared venison demi-glace
½   cup heavy cream
     Fresh rosemary, thyme and white
     pepper to taste

▲ Sauté ½ teaspoon of the shallots in the butter in a saucepan until soft. Add the wine.

▲ Cook over medium heat until the liquid is reduced by half. Add the mushrooms and the remaining shallots. Cook until the shallots are tender.

▲ Add the demi-glace, stirring well to incorporate. Stir in the cream gradually. Season with the rosemary, thyme and white pepper.

▲ Simmer over very low heat until heated through, stirring frequently.

Serves 4

Oven-Fried Catfish

Ann Cox, Kroger Food Stores

4   catfish fillets (about 1½ pounds)
½   cup finely crushed crackers
¼   cup grated Parmesan cheese
1   tablespoon lemon pepper
1   egg white
1   tablespoon water or malt vinegar

▲ Rinse the fillets and pat dry.

▲ Combine the cracker crumbs, Parmesan cheese and lemon pepper in a medium bowl; mix well.

▲ Beat the egg white with the water in a small bowl. Dip the fillets in the egg white mixture; coat with the cracker crumb mixture. Arrange the fillets on a baking sheet sprayed with nonstick cooking spray. Spray the surface of the fillets with the cooking spray.

▲ Bake at 500 degrees for 12 minutes or until the fish flakes easily.

Serves 4

Broiled Orange Roughy

Ann Cox, Kroger Food Stores

6   orange roughy fillets
    Salt, pepper and garlic powder to taste
4   to 6 tablespoons melted butter or margarine
2   tablespoons sherry
2   to 3 tablespoons orange juice
½   to ¾ cup Italian-seasoned bread crumbs

▲ Rinse the fillets and pat dry. Season with the salt, pepper and garlic powder. Arrange in a baking pan.

▲ Combine the butter, sherry and orange juice in a small bowl, mixing well. Pour half of the mixture over the fillets. Mix the remaining mixture with the bread crumbs. Sprinkle over the fillets, covering well.

▲ Broil for 6 to 8 minutes or until the fish flakes easily. Do not turn. Garnish with grated orange peel.

Serves 6

Baked Tilapia

Jack Favier, Executive Chef, Baptist Hospital

4 (6-ounce) tilapia fillets
1 cup milk
½ teaspoon salt
½ teaspoon pepper
1 cup Shake'n Bake
¼ cup melted butter

▲ Rinse the fillets and pat dry.

▲ Combine the milk, salt and pepper in a shallow bowl. Add the fillets. Marinate for 30 minutes in the refrigerator. Drain, discarding the marinade.

▲ Coat the fillets with the Shake'n Bake. Arrange on a baking sheet. Drizzle with the melted butter.

▲ Bake at 350 degrees for 8 to 10 minutes or until the fish flakes easily. Serve with Belgian carrots and oven-roasted new potatoes.

Serves 4

Caribbean Smoked Fish Pie

A Friend of **Talk of the Town**

1 cup flaked smoked fish
1 green bell pepper, chopped
2 cloves garlic, minced
½ cup chopped onion
1 cup tomato purée
½ teaspoon salt (optional)
1 teaspoon hot pepper sauce
1 teaspoon fresh lime juice
1 egg, beaten
1 (9-inch) unbaked pie shell

▲ Combine the fish, green pepper, garlic, onion, tomato purée, salt, pepper sauce and lime juice in a bowl; mix well. Stir in the beaten egg. Pour into the pie shell.

▲ Bake at 375 degrees for 35 minutes or until the filling is set.

Serves 4 to 6

Baked Salmon with Papaya Salsa

Al Anderson, Jamaica Restaurant

Papaya Salsa

1	papaya, peeled, seeded, chopped
1	tablespoon chopped red onion
1	tablespoon chopped red bell pepper
1	tablespoon chopped green bell pepper
1	tablespoon chopped cilantro
½	habanero (Scotch bonnet) chile pepper, chopped
	Juice of 1 lime
1	tablespoon cider vinegar
2	tablespoons pineapple juice
2	tablespoons dark rum

▲ Combine the papaya, onion, bell peppers, cilantro and chile pepper in a medium bowl.

▲ Add the lime juice, vinegar, pineapple juice and rum, mixing well.

▲ Let stand for several hours to blend the flavors.

Baked Salmon

2	tablespoons Dijon mustard
2	tablespoons chopped chipotle
2	tablespoons catsup
1	teaspoon minced garlic
1	teaspoon molasses
¼	cup cider vinegar
1	tablespoon Worcestershire sauce
	Juice of 1 lime
¾	cup olive oil
	Salt and pepper to taste
2	salmon steaks

▲ Combine the mustard, chipotle, catsup, garlic, molasses, vinegar, Worcestershire sauce and lime juice in a food processor container. Process until puréed.

▲ Add the olive oil in a thin stream, continuing to process until the mixture is smooth. Season with salt and pepper.

▲ Rinse the salmon steaks and pat dry. Place in a baking dish. Pour the sauce over the steaks.

▲ Bake at 350 degrees for 10 to 15 minutes or until the fish flakes easily. Remove to warmed serving plates.

▲ Serve with the Papaya Salsa.

Serves 2

TASTE OF **5** THE TOWN

Caraway-Crusted Grilled Salmon
with Pineapple and Green Tomato Salsa

Richard Gerst, Opryland Hotel

Pineapple and Green Tomato Salsa

2   cloves garlic, minced
2   tablespoons chopped shallots
½   tablespoon chopped jalapeño
1   tablespoon extra-virgin olive oil
½   cup fresh orange juice
¼   cup chopped fresh pineapple
¼   cup chopped green tomato
1   tablespoon chopped red
    bell pepper
1   teaspoon vinegar
½   teaspoon curry powder

▲ Sauté the garlic, shallots and jalapeño in the olive oil in a medium skillet until the shallots are translucent; drain well. Add the orange juice.

▲ Bring the mixture to a boil. Cook until the liquid is reduced by half. Add the pineapple, green tomato, red pepper and vinegar.

▲ Cook until heated through. Stir in the curry powder.

Caraway-Crusted Grilled Salmon

4   (4-ounce) salmon fillets
½   teaspoon finely chopped
    caraway seeds
2   cloves garlic, minced
1   tablespoon extra-virgin olive oil

▲ Rinse the salmon and pat dry. Place in a shallow dish.

▲ Combine the caraway seeds, garlic and olive oil in a small bowl. Brush the mixture over the salmon. Marinate in the refrigerator for 25 minutes. Place the salmon on a grill rack.

▲ Grill over hot coals or broil for 6 to 8 minutes or until the salmon flakes easily.

▲ Remove to warmed serving plates. Serve with Pineapple and Green Tomato Salsa.

Serves 4

Cedar-Planked Salmon

Kevin Broege, Regal Maxwell House Hotel

1 (6-ounce) skinned salmon fillet
3 tablespoons maple syrup
4 to 5 pink peppercorns, crushed
1 sprig of fresh thyme, rubbed
  Salt and lemon juice to taste
¼ cup julienned red, green and
  yellow bell peppers
1 tablespoon clarified butter

▲ Rinse the salmon and pat dry. Brush with 1 tablespoon of the maple syrup. Top with the peppercorns, thyme, salt and lemon juice. Place on a 3x6-inch cedar plank.

▲ Bake at 350 degrees for 8 to 10 minutes or until the salmon flakes easily.

▲ Sauté the bell peppers in the butter in a skillet until tender. Stir in the remaining maple syrup. Spoon over the salmon.

▲ Place the salmon on the plank on a serving plate. Garnish with fresh thyme.

Serves 1

Trout with Lemon Dill Sauce

*A Friend of **Talk of the Town***

1 to 2 tablespoons clarified butter
1 fresh trout, cleaned
1 clove garlic, crushed
  Juice of 1 lemon
  Chopped fresh dill, salt and
  pepper to taste

▲ Brush a baking pan with some of the butter. Place the trout skin side down in the pan. Brush the trout with the remaining butter. Rub with the crushed garlic. Sprinkle with the lemon juice and dill. Season with salt and pepper.

▲ Bake at 350 degrees for 5 to 7 minutes or until the trout flakes easily.

Serves 1

Curried Shrimp and Chicken

David Swett, Swett's Restaurant

2 ounces chopped carrots

2 ounces chopped celery

2 ounces chopped onion

4 tablespoons margarine

1 tablespoon curry powder

2 tablespoons flour

1 quart chicken stock

1 tablespoon sugar

2 tablespoons lemon juice

1 tablespoon Tabasco sauce, or to taste

Pinch of salt

1 ounce shredded coconut (optional)

1 skinless boneless chicken breast, cut into bite-sized pieces

10 to 12 jumbo shrimp, shelled, deveined

▲ Sauté the carrots, celery and onion in 2 tablespoons of the margarine in a large skillet. Stir in the curry powder and flour. Add the chicken stock gradually, stirring until flour is blended.

▲ Add the sugar, lemon juice, Tabasco sauce, salt and coconut.

▲ Bring to a boil; reduce heat. Simmer until of desired consistency, stirring frequently.

▲ Rinse the chicken and pat dry. Sauté the shrimp and chicken in the remaining margarine until cooked through. Add to the sauce, stirring to coat. Serve with rice.

Serves 2

Shrimp Scampi

Will Greenwood, Sunset Grill

3 tablespoons olive oil

36 large shrimp, peeled, deveined

¼ cup chopped shallots

2 tablespoons minced garlic

⅓ cup sliced mushrooms

⅓ cup chopped tomatoes

1 cup dry white wine

⅓ cup beef stock or consommé

1 tablespoon cornstarch

1 tablespoon cold water

▲ Heat the olive oil in a large skillet over medium-high heat. Add the shrimp.

▲ Sauté until the shrimp turn pink. Add the shallots and garlic.

▲ Sauté for 30 seconds. Add the mushrooms, tomatoes, wine and beef stock.

▲ Mix the cornstarch and cold water in a bowl, forming a paste. Add to the skillet, stirring until incorporated.

▲ Simmer for 2 to 3 minutes or until the sauce is thickened, stirring frequently.

▲ Serve with rice and bread.

Serves 4 to 6

Pineapple Barbecue Shrimp

Jim Wright

1 teaspoon salt

½ cup sugar

½ cup packed brown sugar

3 cups pineapple juice

½ cup prepared mustard

½ cup liquid smoke

1½ cups catsup

⅓ cup Worcestershire sauce

½ teaspoon red pepper flakes

1 tablespoon chili powder

2 tablespoons chopped chives

2 to 3 pounds jumbo shrimp

1 pound sliced bacon

▲ Combine the salt, sugar, brown sugar and pineapple juice in a saucepan, mixing well. Add the mustard, liquid smoke, catsup, Worcestershire sauce, red pepper flakes, chili powder and chives.

▲ Simmer over medium heat for 20 minutes, stirring occasionally. May thicken sauce with cornstarch if desired.

▲ Peel and devein the shrimp. Wrap each shrimp in a slice of bacon, securing with a wooden pick. Place on a baking pan. Brush with some of the pineapple sauce.

▲ Bake at 425 degrees for 15 to 20 minutes or until the bacon is crisp, turning once. Serve with remaining pineapple sauce.

Serves 4 to 6

Shrimp Rémoulade with Vegetable Rice Timbales

Doc Holliday

Shrimp Rémoulade Sauce

1   to 2 pounds shrimp
1   tablespoon salt
½   cup finely chopped onion
2   cups mayonnaise
1   tablespoon mixed chopped parsley,
     tarragon, chervil and chives
1   tablespoon mustard
2   tablespoons capers, chopped
2   tablespoons chopped sweet pickles

▲ Peel and devein the shrimp. Bring the salt and 1 quart water to a boil in a large saucepan. Add the shrimp.

▲ Cook for 2 to 5 minutes or until the shrimp turn pink. Plunge the shrimp into ice water to stop cooking. Drain and chill in the refrigerator.

▲ Combine the onion, mayonnaise, mixed herbs and mustard in a medium bowl. Squeeze all moisture from the capers and pickles. Stir into the mixture. Chill in the refrigerator. Add the shrimp just before serving.

Red Sauce

1   clove garlic, minced
6   tablespoons catsup
1½ teaspoons prepared horseradish
     Dash of Worcestershire sauce
     Dash of lemon juice

▲ Mix the garlic, catsup, horseradish, Worcestershire sauce and lemon juice in a small bowl.

▲ Chill until serving time.

Rice Timbales

1   cup rice
     Salt to taste
2½ cups water
1   tablespoon butter
1   egg plus 3 egg yolks
½   teaspoon salt
1¼ cups scalded milk
1   cup mixed julienned vegetables

▲ Prepare rice with butter using package directions.

▲ Beat the egg, egg yolks and salt in a bowl. Whisk in the scalded milk. Pour enough of the mixture over the rice to moisten it. Fold in the julienned vegetables. Pack the rice mixture into buttered timbale molds. Place in a baking pan filled with water to come halfway up the side of the timbales.

▲ Bake at 325 degrees for 30 minutes or until the mixture is firm. Serve with the Shrimp Rémoulade Sauce and Red Sauce on the side.

Serves 4 to 6

Ann's Crab Cakes with Mustard Sauce

Ann Cox, Kroger Food Stores

Crab Cakes

8 ounces fresh crab meat
1 cup fine dry bread crumbs
1 tablespoon Worcestershire sauce
1 tablespoon prepared horseradish
1 tablespoon lemon juice
1 tablespoon Dijon mustard
1 egg
1 teaspoon Old Bay seasoning
¼ cup light mayonnaise
⅓ cup chopped green onions
1 teaspoon chopped parsley
¼ teaspoon red pepper flakes
2 tablespoons olive oil

▲ Combine the crab meat, ½ cup of the bread crumbs, Worcestershire sauce, horseradish, lemon juice, Dijon mustard, egg, Old Bay seasoning, mayonnaise, green onions, parsley and red pepper flakes in a bowl; mix well.

▲ Shape into 2½-inch patties. Coat with the remaining bread crumbs.

▲ Heat the olive oil in a large skillet. Sauté the crab cakes on each side until golden brown.

Mustard Sauce

¼ cup light mayonnaise
1 tablespoon plus 1 teaspoon Dijon mustard with horseradish, or to taste
1 tablespoon plus 1 teaspoon stone-ground mustard, or to taste

▲ Mix the mayonnaise, Dijon mustard with horseradish and stone-ground mustard in a small bowl.

▲ Serve in a small dish to accompany the crab cakes.

Serves 4 to 6

Maryland Crab Cakes

Craig Jervis, The Mad Platter

2 pounds crab meat, drained, flaked

½ cup finely chopped red
   bell pepper

2 tablespoons blackening spice

2 cups mayonnaise

   Juice of 3 lemons

¾ cup minced onion, rinsed

1½ cups dry bread crumbs

2 to 4 tablespoons margarine

▲ Combine the crab meat, red pepper, blackening spice, mayonnaise, lemon juice and onion in a bowl. Add the bread crumbs gradually, mixing well.

▲ Shape the mixture into patties, squeezing out excess moisture.

▲ Heat the margarine in a skillet over medium heat until the margarine melts and begins to sizzle. Add the patties.

▲ Cook the patties until cooked through and browned on each side. Garnish with lemon slices and serve with green beans and rice.

Serves 12

 Always use your fingers to pick over fresh or canned crab meat to make sure there are no tiny pieces of shell.

Crawfish Cakes with Key Lime Mustard Sauce

Al Anderson, Jamaica Restaurant

Key Lime Mustard Sauce

2   cups mayonnaise

¼   cup Key lime juice

2   tablespoons Worcestershire sauce

¼   cup Dijon mustard

2   tablespoons Tabasco sauce

▲ Combine the mayonnaise, lime juice, Worcestershire sauce, Dijon mustard and Tabasco sauce in a small bowl; mix well. Chill until serving time.

Crawfish Cakes

1   pound cooked crawfish tails with fat

1   red bell pepper, chopped

1   egg

1   tablespoon Worcestershire sauce

1   cup mayonnaise

2   tablespoons seafood magic

1   bunch green onions, chopped

    Juice of 3 lemons

1   tablespoon Tabasco sauce

¼   cup cracker meal

    Dry bread crumbs

2   tablespoons butter

▲ Mix the crawfish, red pepper, egg, Worcestershire sauce, mayonnaise, seafood magic, green onions, lemon juice, Tabasco sauce and cracker meal in a large bowl. Add enough bread crumbs to make a firm mixture that holds together. Shape the mixture into patties.

▲ Melt the butter in a large skillet. Add the patties. Cook until brown on each side. Serve with Key Lime Mustard Sauce.

Serves 4 to 6

Seafood Basil Pasta à la Hummell

Kala MacLeod & Art Victorine for Pasta Premier

½ cup extra-virgin olive oil

⅓ cup pine nuts

4 cloves garlic, minced

2 cups fresh basil leaves

1 pound salmon fillet, skinned, grilled

1 pound bay scallops, cooked

1 pound linguini, cooked

▲ Combine the olive oil, pine nuts, garlic and basil in a food processor container. Process until puréed.

▲ Flake the salmon in a large bowl. Add the scallops, linguini and basil purée. Toss gently to coat.

Serves 4 to 6

Pesto, Prawns, Prosciutto and Pasta

Jules Lieb, Jules Dining Hall and Barcar

2 tablespoons minced garlic

¼ cup chopped scallions

2 tablespoons minced shallots

¼ cup shiitake mushrooms

24 large shrimp, peeled, deveined

¼ cup sun-dried tomatoes

3 cups torn fresh spinach

1 cup heavy cream

1 cup shaved prosciutto

¼ cup prepared pesto sauce

1 pound angel hair pasta, cooked

▲ Sauté the garlic, scallions and shallots in a large skillet until tender. Add the mushrooms and shrimp.

▲ Sauté until the shrimp turn pink, stirring frequently. Add the sun-dried tomatoes and spinach.

▲ Cook just until the spinach is slightly wilted. Stir in the cream, prosciutto and pesto sauce.

▲ Simmer over low heat until slightly thickened.

▲ Place pasta in a serving bowl. Add the sauce; toss gently.

Serves 4

Rasta Pasta

Jody Faison, 12th & Porter Restaurant

Blackening Spice

1½	tablespoons salt
1	tablespoon paprika
1	teaspoon onion powder
1	teaspoon garlic powder
1	teaspoon dried thyme
½	teaspoon dried oregano
½	teaspoon pepper
1	teaspoon cayenne

▲ Combine the salt, paprika, onion powder, garlic powder, thyme, oregano, pepper and cayenne in a small bowl; mix well.

Rasta Pasta

1	skinless boneless chicken breast
½	cup Blackening Spice
1	tablespoon olive oil
1	tablespoon freshly chopped garlic
2	ounces green onions, chopped
2	tablespoons olive oil
3	ounces sea scallops
3	ounces bay shrimp
½	cup heavy cream
1	teaspoon mixed salt, pepper and granulated garlic
5	ounces fettuccini, cooked
¼	cup grated Parmesan cheese

▲ Rinse the chicken and pat dry. Coat with the Blackening Spice.

▲ Cook in 1 tablespoon olive oil in a skillet over medium-high heat until cooked through and bright red; set aside.

▲ Sauté the garlic and green onions in 2 tablespoons olive oil in a large skillet for 1 minute. Add the scallops and shrimp.

▲ Sauté for 2 minutes, stirring frequently. Add the heavy cream and mixed salt, pepper and garlic.

▲ Simmer over low heat until the liquid is reduced by half. Add the pasta and Parmesan cheese, tossing to coat. Serve topped with the chicken.

Serves 1

TASTE OF 5 THE TOWN

Spaghetti Al Picchi Pacchio

Caesar Randazzo, Caesar's Restaurant

1	tablespoon butter
1	tablespoon olive oil
2	tablespoons chopped green onions
1	teaspoon minced garlic
5	ounces baby shrimp, peeled
1	cup chopped tomatoes
	Oregano, basil, red pepper flakes and black pepper to taste
1	teaspoon lemon juice
3	ounces dry white wine
8	ounces spaghetti, cooked
1	cup grated Parmesan cheese

▲ Melt the butter with the olive oil in a deep large skillet. Sauté the green onions and garlic for 1 to 2 minutes. Add the shrimp.

▲ Cook over medium heat just until the shrimp turn pink. Add the tomatoes, oregano, basil, red pepper flakes and black pepper. Stir in the lemon juice and wine.

▲ Simmer for 1 to 2 minutes. Pour over the cooked spaghetti in a large bowl. Add the Parmesan cheese gradually, tossing to coat.

Serves 2

Place pasta in a strainer in the saucepan to cook. Lift the strainer from the pan at the end of the cooking time; draining is automatic.

Black-Eyed Pea Pasta

Doc Holliday

1 cup elbow macaroni

5 cups frozen black-eyed peas

1 cup chopped onion

3 cloves garlic, minced

2 tablespoons bacon drippings

1 pound ground beef

1 teaspoon seasoned salt

1½ teaspoons chili seasoning

2 teaspoons garlic salt

½ teaspoon ground oregano

1½ teaspoons sugar

½ teaspoon dried basil

1 teaspoon salt

¼ teaspoon black pepper

1 to 2 tablespoons Worcestershire sauce

2 (16-ounce) cans stewed tomatoes

▲ Cook the macaroni using package directions. Drain and set aside.

▲ Cook the black-eyed peas using package directions. Drain and set aside.

▲ Sauté the onion and garlic in the bacon drippings in a large skillet until the onion is tender. Add the ground beef.

▲ Cook until the ground beef is browned and crumbly, stirring constantly. Add the seasoned salt, chili seasoning, garlic salt, oregano, sugar, basil, salt, pepper, Worcestershire sauce and undrained tomatoes; mix well.

▲ Simmer for 25 minutes, stirring to break up the tomatoes. Add the macaroni and black-eyed peas.

▲ Simmer for 5 minutes longer or until heated through.

Serves 8 to 10

When cooking pasta, add 1 or 2 tablespoons vegetable oil to the cooking water to keep pasta separated.

Smoked Chicken Pasta Pie with Roasted Garlic Alfredo Sauce

Mozzarella's Cafe

Roasted Garlic Alfredo Sauce

6   tablespoons lightly salted butter
¾   cup chopped yellow onion
1   tablespoon minced garlic
6   tablespoons flour
1½ cups chicken stock
3   cups half-and-half
2   teaspoons white pepper
1½ tablespoons fresh lemon juice
1½ tablespoons roasted garlic

▲ Melt the butter in a double boiler. Add the onion and garlic.

▲ Cook until the onion is translucent. Stir in the flour. Cook for 3 minutes to form a roux.

▲ Heat the chicken stock in a small saucepan. Add gradually to the roux, whisking constantly until smooth.

▲ Simmer for 10 minutes. Mix the half-and-half with the white pepper. Stir into the roux.

▲ Bring to a boil; remove from the heat. Strain into a large skillet; discard the onion. Whisk the lemon juice and roasted garlic into the sauce.

Smoked Chicken Pasta Pie

½   cup Roasted Garlic Alfredo Sauce
2   tablespoons grated Parmesan cheese
1   tablespoon butter
2½ cups cooked penne noodles
½   cup (¼ x 2-inch) smoked chicken strips
½   cup sliced mushrooms
5   roasted red bell pepper strips
¾   cup shredded Quatro cheese
1   tablespoon thinly sliced scallions

▲ Heat the Alfredo Sauce, Parmesan cheese and butter in a large skillet; do not boil.

▲ Add the pasta, tossing with a spatula. Spoon into a baking dish. Top with the smoked chicken strips and mushrooms. Arrange the red pepper strips over the top to form a star. Sprinkle with the Quatro cheese.

▲ Bake at 400 degrees until the cheese is melted. Top with the scallions.

Serves 2

TASTE OF **5** THE TOWN

Fettuccini "What's To Cook Tonight"

Jim Hammond, Belle Meade Brasserie and Finezza

Olive oil
½ tablespoon crushed garlic
4 ounces smoked turkey, chopped
1 cup frozen peas
Pinch of nutmeg
Salt and pepper to taste
½ cup dry white wine
1 cup chicken broth
½ cup heavy cream
¼ cup grated Parmesan cheese
1½ pounds fettuccini, cooked

▲ Brush a 10-inch skillet with olive oil. Heat over medium-high heat. Add the garlic, turkey, peas, nutmeg, salt and pepper.

▲ Sauté until the garlic is translucent, stirring frequently. Add the wine, chicken broth and cream.

▲ Bring to a boil, stirring constantly; reduce the heat. Add the Parmesan cheese.

▲ Simmer until the cheese is melted. Add the pasta.

▲ Simmer until the sauce is reduced and thickened. Transfer to a warm plate to serve.

Serves 3

5 For an easy and delicious pasta dish, prepare Sautéed Broccoli Spaghetti. Sauté garlic and chopped broccoli in olive oil, add 1 pound of cooked spaghetti and serve with cheese.

TASTE OF **5** THE TOWN

Mediterranean Pasta

Doc Holliday

8   ounces penne

⅔ cup crumbled feta cheese

¼ cup grated Parmesan cheese

1   medium red onion, sliced

2   tablespoons olive oil

1   (14-ounce) can quartered
    artichoke hearts, rinsed, drained

1   (17-ounce) can crushed tomatoes

1   small red bell pepper, sliced

1   small green bell pepper, sliced

1   (2-ounce) can sliced black olives,
    drained

¼ teaspoon salt

½ teaspoon freshly ground pepper

▲ Cook the pasta using package directions; drain. Place in a lightly greased 7x11-inch baking dish. Sprinkle with half the feta cheese and half the Parmesan cheese; set aside.

▲ Sauté the onion in the olive oil in a large skillet over medium-high heat until the onion is tender. Add the artichokes, undrained tomatoes and bell peppers.

▲ Cook for 2 to 3 minutes, stirring frequently; reduce the heat. Add the black olives, salt and pepper.

▲ Simmer, covered, for 10 minutes. Pour over the penne. Top with the remaining feta cheese and Parmesan cheese.

▲ Bake at 350 degrees for 15 to 20 minutes or until cheese is melted.

Serves 3 to 4

Pasta Feta Delight

Carey Clarke Aron, The Pasta Shoppe

12 ounces pasta

1 cup crumbled feta cheese

⅔ cup loosely packed minced parsley

⅔ cup firmly packed minced fresh basil

3 tomatoes, seeded, coarsely chopped

¼ cup lemon juice

¼ cup extra-virgin olive oil

½ teaspoon salt

¼ teaspoon pepper

▲ Cook the pasta using package directions; drain and rinse with cold water.

▲ Combine with the feta cheese, parsley, basil, tomatoes, lemon juice, olive oil, salt and pepper in a large bowl. Toss gently to coat.

▲ Serve at room temperature or chilled.

Serves 6 to 8

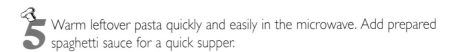 Warm leftover pasta quickly and easily in the microwave. Add prepared spaghetti sauce for a quick supper.

Pasta Yaya

Jody Faison, 12th & Porter Restaurant

5   ounces chicken, sliced

1   tablespoon margarine

½   tablespoon minced garlic

½   cup chopped green onions

3   ounces sausage, cooked, sliced

½   cup heavy cream

½   cup chicken stock

8   ounces pasta, cooked
    Salt and pepper to taste

1   tablespoon Blackening Spice
    (page 128)

▲ Rinse the chicken and pat dry.

▲ Melt the margarine in a large saucepan. Add the garlic and green onions. Sauté for 1 minute. Add the sausage and chicken.

▲ Cook until the chicken is cooked through but not browned. Add the cream.

▲ Simmer over medium-low heat until the liquid is reduced by ⅓. Stir in the chicken stock and pasta.

▲ Simmer until the sauce is thickened slightly, stirring constantly. Season with salt, pepper and Blackening Spice.

Serves 2

 Shaped pasta usually costs more than plain, but is still an economical way to liven up a meal.

St. Patrick's Day Pasta

Luke Belsito, Pargo's Restaurant

½ cup chopped fresh spinach
½ cup cream cheese
½ cup chopped cooked bacon
2 (6-ounce) skinless, boneless chicken breasts
   Seasoned flour
   Olive oil
1 cup chicken stock
1½ cups heavy cream
¼ cup prepared pesto
   Salt and pepper to taste
8 to 10 ounces spinach fettuccini, cooked

▲ Purée the spinach, cream cheese and bacon in a food processor.

▲ Flatten the chicken with a meat mallet. Spread the spinach mixture over the chicken. Roll up to enclose the filling, securing with a wooden pick if necessary. Coat with the seasoned flour.

▲ Cook in the olive oil in a large skillet over medium-high heat until browned. Place in a baking dish.

▲ Bake, covered, at 350 degrees for 15 to 20 minutes or until cooked through.

▲ Deglaze the skillet with the chicken stock. Add the cream, pesto, salt and pepper.

▲ Simmer until the sauce thickens, stirring constantly. Add the fettuccini, tossing to coat. Transfer to serving plates.

▲ Cut the chicken rolls into ¼-inch slices. Arrange over the fettuccini. Garnish with toasted sliced almonds, grated Parmesan cheese and fresh basil leaves.

Serves 2

Spinach Lasagna

Lisa Sheehan-Smith, Baptist Hospital

8   ounces lasagna noodles

1   (10-ounce) package frozen
    chopped spinach, thawed, drained

1   (26-ounce) jar low-fat
    spaghetti sauce

⅔   cup grated Parmesan cheese

2   cups 1% milk-fat cottage cheese

1   egg white

3   cups shredded mozzarella cheese

▲ Cook the lasagna noodles using package directions; drain and set aside.

▲ Mix the spinach and spaghetti sauce in a large bowl.

▲ Combine the Parmesan cheese, cottage cheese and egg white in a small bowl; mix well.

▲ Spray a 9x13-inch baking dish with nonstick cooking spray. Layer ⅓ of the noodles, ⅓ of the spinach mixture, half the cottage cheese mixture and ½ cup of the mozzarella cheese in the prepared dish. Layer half the remaining noodles, half the remaining spinach mixture, remaining cottage cheese and half the remaining mozzarella cheese over layers. Layer the remaining noodles, remaining spinach and remaining mozzarella cheese over the top.

▲ Bake, uncovered, at 350 degrees for 30 to 40 minutes or until bubbly.

Serves 12

Italian Non-Meatballs

Marilyn White, Natural Lifestyles

½ cup finely chopped pecans

½ cup shredded skim mozzarella cheese

½ medium onion, finely chopped

Dash of salt

1 clove garlic, chopped

1 cup cracker crumbs

4 egg whites, beaten

1 teaspoon sage

2 tablespoons parsley flakes

Olive oil

▲ Combine the pecans, mozzarella cheese, onion, salt, garlic, cracker crumbs, egg whites, sage and parsley flakes in a bowl; mix well. Shape the mixture into 12 small balls.

▲ Sauté in olive oil in a skillet over medium-high heat until browned.

▲ Simmer with your favorite spaghetti sauce for 25 to 45 minutes. Serve over spaghetti.

Serves 3 to 4

 Shape uniform meatballs by using a small ice cream scoop.

Chapter 6

Breads

Ruth Ann Leach talks with Senator Al Gore, Jr. in the early 1980s on Job-A-Thon.

NewsChannel**5**

The NewsChannel 5
Weather Team:
Lelan Statom, Ron Howes,
and Joe Case.

NewsChannel 5 favorites
Bill Jay and Bob Lobertini
are seen here in their roles as
Captain Bob and Captain Bill on
"Popeye" in 1959.

Apricot-Coconut Bread

Doc Holliday

¾ cup butter, softened

¾ cup sugar

2   eggs, beaten

¾ cup chopped dried apricots

½ cup shredded unsweetened coconut

¼ cup fresh orange juice

1   teaspoon grated orange peel

1½ cups whole wheat flour

1½ cups all-purpose flour

1   teaspoon salt

1   teaspoon baking soda

1   cup buttermilk

½ cup chopped walnuts

▲ Cream the butter and sugar in a large mixer bowl until light and fluffy. Add the eggs, beating well. Fold in the apricots, coconut, orange juice and orange peel.

▲ Sift the whole wheat flour and all-purpose flour together with the salt and baking soda. Add to the apricot mixture alternately with the buttermilk. Fold in the walnuts. Pour the batter into a greased 5x9-inch loaf pan.

▲ Bake at 350 degrees for 1 hour or until the loaf tests done. Cool in the pan for 10 minutes; invert onto a wire rack to cool completely.

Serves 9

5 Use kitchen shears to snip dried fruit like apples, apricots and dates. Dip the shears in hot water or granulated sugar every so often to keep the fruit from sticking.

Chocolate Zucchini Bread

Ann Cox, Kroger Food Stores

1   cup vegetable oil
2   eggs
2   cups sugar
2   teaspoons vanilla extract
1   teaspoon baking soda
2½ cups flour
¼   teaspoon baking powder
1   teaspoon salt
1   tablespoon cinnamon
3   tablespoons (heaping) baking cocoa
2   cups grated zucchini
1   cup chopped pecans

▲ Beat the oil and eggs in a mixer bowl. Add the sugar, vanilla, baking soda, flour, baking powder, salt, cinnamon and baking cocoa; mix well. Fold in the zucchini and pecans. Pour into two 4x8-inch loaf pans sprayed with nonstick cooking spray.

▲ Bake at 350 degrees for 50 to 60 minutes or until the loaves test done. Cool in the pans for 5 minutes; invert onto wire racks to cool completely.

Serves 16

 Most breads will stay fresh for 5 to 7 days at room temperature if wrapped airtight.

Bacon Cheese Bread

Lynne Tolley, Miss Mary Bobo's Boarding House

4   slices bacon

¼   cup chopped green onions

2   tablespoons freshly chopped
    parsley

2   cups flour

2   teaspoons baking powder

2   teaspoons dry mustard

½   teaspoon salt

1   cup milk

2   eggs, beaten

1   cup shredded Jarlsberg cheese

▲ Cook the bacon in a skillet until crispy. Remove bacon from skillet and crumble. Sauté the green onions and parsley in the bacon drippings until the green onions are tender. Remove from the heat and set aside.

▲ Combine the flour, baking powder, dry mustard and salt in a large bowl.

▲ Beat the milk and eggs in a small bowl. Stir into the dry ingredients. Add the undrained green onion mixture, stirring just until moistened. Stir in the crumbled bacon and cheese. Pour into a greased 5x9-inch loaf pan.

▲ Bake at 375 degrees for 1 hour or until the loaf tests done. Cool in the pan for 10 minutes; invert onto a wire rack to cool completely.

Serves 9

5 Spread slices of French bread with butter seasoned with parsley, chopped green onions, thyme, marjoram and garlic powder. Bake in foil at 400 degrees for 10 to 15 minutes.

Farm Pumpkin Bread

Daisy King, **Miss Daisy Celebrates Tennessee**

1	cup water
3	eggs
1	cup vegetable oil
1	(16-ounce) can pumpkin
3	cups sugar
1	cup chopped black walnuts
1½	cups chopped dates
3½	cups self-rising flour
1	teaspoon each salt, ginger and nutmeg
2	teaspoons cinnamon
½	teaspoon ground cloves
½	teaspoon baking powder
2	teaspoons baking soda

▲ Combine the water, eggs, oil, pumpkin and sugar in a large bowl; beat until smooth. Fold in the walnuts and dates.

▲ Sift the flour, salt, ginger, nutmeg, cinnamon, cloves, baking powder and baking soda together. Add to the pumpkin mixture, stirring until moistened. Pour into 2 greased 5x9-inch loaf pans.

▲ Bake at 325 degrees for 1½ hours or until the loaves test done. Cool in the pan for 5 minutes; invert onto wire racks to cool completely.

Serves 16

Pumpkin Bread Roll

Ann Cox, Tennessee Egg and Poultry Association

3	eggs
1	cup sugar
⅔	cup canned pumpkin
1	teaspoon lemon juice
1	teaspoon baking powder
¾	cup flour
2	teaspoons cinnamon
1	teaspoon ground ginger
½	teaspoon each nutmeg and salt
	Confectioners' sugar

▲ Beat the eggs and sugar in a mixer bowl until light and fluffy. Add the pumpkin and lemon juice, beating until smooth.

▲ Sift the baking powder, flour, cinnamon, ginger, nutmeg and salt together. Fold into the pumpkin mixture, stirring until moistened. Spread the batter over the bottom of an 11x16-inch jellyroll pan.

▲ Bake at 375 degrees for 15 minutes. Invert onto a towel. Sprinkle with confectioners' sugar. Roll up the bread in the towel. Chill in the refrigerator. Unroll, removing the towel. Reroll and place on a serving plate. Sprinkle with additional confectioners' sugar.

Serves 10

Sour Cream Cherry Walnut Bread

Ethel Minor, Tennessee State Fair Winner

½ cup sugar

½ cup packed light brown sugar

½ cup butter or margarine, softened

1 cup light or nonfat sour cream

3 eggs

2½ cups flour

1 teaspoon (scant) salt

1 tablespoon baking powder

½ teaspoon baking soda

2 teaspoons rum extract

2 teaspoons maraschino cherry extract

½ cup maraschino cherry juice

1½ cups roasted chopped walnuts

1½ cups chopped maraschino cherries

▲ Cream the sugar, brown sugar, butter, sour cream and eggs in a large mixer bowl until light and fluffy. Add the flour, salt, baking powder, baking soda, rum extract, cherry extract and cherry juice. Beat at low speed for 15 seconds. Beat at medium speed for 30 seconds, scraping the side of the bowl. Fold in the walnuts and cherries.

▲ Grease the bottom of two 2-pound loaf pans. Pour in the batter.

▲ Bake at 350 degrees for 70 to 75 minutes or until the loaves test done.

▲ Loosen the loaves from the sides of the pans. Remove to wire racks to cool completely. Wrap in plastic wrap and chill for 8 hours before slicing.

▲ Garnish with whole walnuts, red cherry halves and green cherry slivers brushed with corn syrup.

Serves 16

 Make bread pudding out of unusual breads such as raisin bread, coffee cake, sweet rolls or croissants.

Potato Dill Biscuits

Connie Cahill, Colorado Potatoes

1   medium Colorado potato,
    peeled, chopped
½   cup water
2   cups flour
1   tablespoon baking powder
2   teaspoons sugar
1   teaspoon dried dillweed
½   teaspoon cream of tartar
½   teaspoon salt
¼   cup shortening
¼   cup butter

▲ Combine the potato and water in a small saucepan. Cook, covered, over medium heat for 10 minutes or until the potato is tender. Do not drain. Mash until very smooth or purée in a blender. Spoon into a glass measure, adding additional water to measure 1 cup.

▲ Combine the flour, baking powder, sugar, dillweed, cream of tartar and salt in a large bowl. Cut in the shortening and butter until the mixture is crumbly. Add the potato mixture, stirring until the batter is slightly sticky.

▲ Knead on a lightly floured surface 10 to 12 times. Shape into an 8-inch square. Cut into 16 equal squares. Place on a baking sheet.

▲ Bake at 450 degrees for 10 to 12 minutes or until lightly browned.

Serves 16

5 Cut out biscuits, place on a baking sheet and brush with milk. Freeze until firm. Place in a plastic bag in the freezer until needed. Bake as usual without thawing.

Sweet Potato Biscuits

Penny DeWeese, Miss Penny's

2 cups sifted flour
4 teaspoons baking powder
1 teaspoon salt
⅔ cup shortening
1 cup cooked, mashed sweet potatoes
3 tablespoons milk

▲ Sift the flour, baking powder and salt into a large bowl. Cut in the shortening until crumbly. Add the sweet potatoes and milk, stirring until a soft dough forms. Knead lightly. Roll out to a ¾-inch thickness on a lightly floured surface.

▲ Cut into 2-inch circles. Place on an ungreased baking sheet.

▲ Bake at 375 degrees for 20 minutes or until browned.

Serves 20

Coconut Crescents

Doc Holliday

⅓ cup sugar
1 cup melted butter
1 teaspoon vanilla extract
2 cups flour
7 ounces shredded sweetened coconut
½ cup chopped pecans

▲ Combine the sugar, butter, vanilla, flour and coconut in a large bowl. Stir until a soft dough forms. Fold in the pecans.

▲ Shape into 2-inch crescents. Place on an ungreased baking sheet.

▲ Bake at 350 degrees for 30 minutes or until golden brown. Cool before serving.

▲ May store for up to one week in an airtight container.

Serves 12

TASTE OF **5** THE TOWN

Rocky Mountain Icebox Rolls

Connie Cahill, Colorado Potatoes

1	envelope active dry yeast
¼	cup lukewarm water
½	cup sugar
1	egg
3	tablespoons shortening
1	cup Colorado potatoes, mashed
2	cups hot water
1	teaspoon salt
6	to 7 cups flour

▲ Dissolve the yeast in the lukewarm water; set aside.

▲ Beat the sugar, egg and shortening in a large mixer bowl. Add the potatoes, hot water, salt and 1 cup of the flour; mix well. Stir in the yeast mixture and the remaining flour gradually until a stiff dough forms.

▲ Cover with a towel and let rise until doubled in bulk. Punch down. Store in the refrigerator to use as needed.

▲ To bake, shape the dough into rolls and let rise until doubled in bulk. Place on a baking sheet.

▲ Bake at 350 degrees for 20 to 25 minutes or until lightly browned.

Serves 24 to 30

Refrigerator Rolls

Judy Ratliff Powell, Holly Berry Inn

2	envelopes active dry yeast
¼	cup warm water
1	quart milk
1	cup sugar
1	cup shortening
8	cups flour
1	tablespoon salt
½	teaspoon baking soda

▲ Dissolve the yeast in the warm water; set aside.

▲ Scald the milk in a saucepan. Combine with the sugar and shortening in a large bowl. Stir in the yeast mixture.

▲ Sift the flour, salt and baking soda together. Add to the yeast mixture, stirring until a stiff dough forms.

▲ Cover and let rise until doubled in bulk; punch down. Chill for several hours. Roll out the dough and shape into rolls. Place on a baking sheet. Let rise until doubled in bulk.

▲ Bake at 350 degrees for 15 minutes or until browned.

Serves 30 to 40

Healthier Version of Joe Case's Killer Kornbread

Donna Gurchiek, Baptist Hospital

1   (8-ounce) can cream-style corn
1   cup plain nonfat yogurt
4   egg whites
2   teaspoons canola oil
1   cup self-rising cornmeal
1   teaspoon baking powder
2   teaspoons sugar

▲ Preheat a large greased cast-iron skillet in a 400-degree oven.

▲ Combine the corn, yogurt, egg whites, canola oil, cornmeal, baking powder and sugar in a large bowl; mix well. Pour into the hot skillet.

▲ Bake at 400 degrees for 25 to 30 minutes or until browned. Let stand for 5 minutes before serving.

Serves 8 to 10

Potato Parmesan Muffins

Connie Cahill, Colorado Potatoes

1   medium Colorado potato, peeled, coarsely chopped
½   cup water
¼   cup milk
¼   cup vegetable oil
1   egg, beaten
1⅔ cups flour
3   tablespoons sugar
2   teaspoons baking powder
½   teaspoon crushed dried basil
¼   teaspoon baking soda
¼   cup grated Parmesan cheese

▲ Cook the potato in ½ cup water in a small saucepan over medium heat for 10 minutes or until tender. Do not drain. Mash in a medium bowl until smooth. Stir in enough of the milk to measure 1 cup; let cool slightly. Beat in the oil and egg.

▲ Combine the flour, sugar, baking powder, basil, baking soda and ½ of the Parmesan cheese in a large bowl. Add the potato mixture, beating until moistened.

▲ Spoon into greased or paper-lined muffin cups. Sprinkle with the remaining Parmesan cheese.

▲ Bake at 400 degrees for 20 minutes or until lightly browned. Remove from the pan and cool on a wire rack.

Serves 12

Spiced Whole Wheat Muffins

Doc Holliday

2⅔ cups sifted all-purpose flour

1⅓ cups whole wheat flour

1 teaspoon ground cinnamon

½ teaspoon ground ginger

¼ teaspoon ground allspice

4 teaspoons baking powder

1½ teaspoons salt

¼ cup raisins

¼ cup chopped pecans

3 eggs, beaten

¼ cup molasses or honey

1½ to 1¾ cups milk

¼ cup melted butter

▲ Combine the all-purpose flour, whole wheat flour, cinnamon, ginger, allspice, baking powder, salt, raisins and pecans in a large bowl.

▲ Beat the eggs, molasses, milk and butter in a small bowl. Add to the dry ingredients, stirring just until moistened. The dough will be slightly lumpy, but do not overmix.

▲ Spray muffin cups with nonstick cooking spray. Spoon the batter into the muffin cups, filling ⅔ full.

▲ Bake at 400 degrees for 20 to 25 minutes or until the muffins test done. Remove to a wire rack to cool.

Serves 24

 Add 1 cup chopped prunes, dried apricots, raisins or figs to your favorite muffin recipe.

Carrot Nut Pancakes

Andrea Beaudet, Hillsboro House Bed and Breakfast

1½ cups flour

1   teaspoon baking powder

½   teaspoon salt

½   teaspoon baking soda

2   tablespoons sugar

½   teaspoon ground cinnamon

2   eggs

1   cup buttermilk

2   tablespoons vegetable oil or melted butter

½   cup grated carrots

½   cup chopped pecans

▲ Sift the flour, baking powder, salt, baking soda, sugar and cinnamon into a large bowl.

▲ Beat the eggs in a medium bowl. Add the buttermilk, mixing well. Stir into the sifted dry ingredients. Add the oil, beating well. Fold in the carrots and pecans. Let stand for 1 hour.

▲ Oil a skillet or griddle and heat over medium heat. Pour 2 tablespoons of the batter into the skillet. Cook until bubbles appear. Turn and cook on the other side. Repeat with the remaining batter.

Serves 12 to 15

5 Bake pancakes and cool. Freeze in serving portions in plastic bags. Reheat, wrapped in moist paper towel, at 200 degrees or microwave on High for 20 seconds per pancake.

After the Opry Coffee Cake

Martha Sundquist, First Lady of Tennessee

½ cup sugar

3 ounces cream cheese, softened

¼ cup butter, softened

1 egg

1 teaspoon vanilla extract

1 cup self-rising flour

¼ cup milk

1 teaspoon grated lemon peel

½ jar Raspberry Butter (about 5 ounces)

½ cup confectioners' sugar

1 tablespoon lemon juice

1 tablespoon butter, softened

¼ cup chopped pecans

▲ Cream the sugar, cream cheese, butter, egg and vanilla in a mixer bowl until light and fluffy. Add the flour, milk and lemon peel, beating at low speed until moistened. Beat at medium speed for 2 minutes longer.

▲ Spread the batter into a greased and floured 8-inch springform pan. Spoon the Raspberry Butter 1 teaspoon at a time over the batter. Swirl with a knife to marbleize.

▲ Bake at 350 degrees for 25 to 30 minutes or until a knife inserted near the center comes out clean. Cool slightly. Remove the side from the pan.

▲ Beat the confectioners' sugar, lemon juice and 1 tablespoon butter in a small mixer bowl until smooth. Spread over the coffee cake. Sprinkle with the pecans. Serve warm.

Serves 8

 Substitute 1 cup all-purpose flour, 1 teaspoon baking powder and ½ teaspoon salt for 1 cup self-rising flour.

Quick and Easy Coffee Cake

Doc Holliday

½ cup butter
½ cup chopped pecans or walnuts
2 (8-count) cans refrigerated crescent rolls
1 cup packed brown sugar
2 tablespoons water

▲ Melt the butter in a small saucepan. Coat the bottom and side of an 8-inch square baking pan with 2 tablespoons of the butter. Sprinkle the pan with 3 tablespoons of the pecans.

▲ Remove dough from cans in rolled sections. Cut each section into 4 slices. Arrange in the prepared pan, leaving a small space between each pinwheel.

▲ Combine the remaining pecans, brown sugar and water with the remaining butter in the saucepan. Bring to a boil, stirring frequently. Pour over the pinwheels.

▲ Bake at 375 degrees for 25 to 30 minutes or until golden brown. Cool in the pan for 3 minutes. Invert onto a serving platter to serve.

Serves 8 to 10

Raspberry Coffee Cake

Doc Holliday

1 cup butter, softened
4 eggs
1½ cups sifted flour
½ cup sugar
½ cup packed light brown sugar
2 teaspoons baking powder
   Pinch of salt
1 (10-ounce) package frozen raspberries in syrup, thawed, drained
½ cup chopped pecans
1 cup flour
½ cup melted butter
⅓ cup packed light brown sugar
1 teaspoon ground cinnamon

▲ Cream 1 cup butter in a large mixer bowl until light and fluffy. Add the eggs 1 at a time, beating well at low speed after each addition.

▲ Combine 1½ cups flour, ½ cup sugar, ½ cup brown sugar, baking powder and salt in a medium bowl. Add to the creamed mixture. Beat at low speed for 6 minutes.

▲ Pour the batter into a buttered 9x13-inch baking pan. Cover with the raspberries; sprinkle with the pecans.

▲ Mix 1 cup flour, melted butter, ⅓ cup brown sugar and cinnamon in a small bowl. Spoon over the raspberries and pecans.

▲ Bake at 350 degrees for 35 to 40 minutes or until golden brown. Cool slightly before serving.

Serves 6 to 8

Raspberry-Almond Coffee Cake

Mackenzie Colt

1	cup fresh raspberries
3	tablespoons brown sugar
1	cup flour
½	cup sugar
½	teaspoon baking powder
¼	teaspoon baking soda
⅛	teaspoon salt
½	cup plain low-fat yogurt
2	tablespoons melted margarine
1	teaspoon vanilla extract
1	egg
1	tablespoon sliced almonds
¼	cup sifted confectioners' sugar
1	teaspoon skim milk
¼	teaspoon vanilla extract

▲ Toss the raspberries with the brown sugar in a small bowl; set aside.

▲ Combine the flour, sugar, baking powder, baking soda and salt in a large bowl.

▲ Beat the yogurt, margarine, 1 teaspoon vanilla and egg in a medium bowl until smooth. Add to the dry ingredients, stirring until moistened.

▲ Spoon ⅔ of the batter into an 8-inch round baking pan sprayed with nonstick cooking spray. Top with the raspberries. Spoon the remaining batter over the raspberries. Sprinkle with the almonds.

▲ Bake at 350 degrees for 40 minutes or until a wooden pick inserted near the center comes out clean. Cool for 10 minutes.

▲ Combine the confectioners' sugar, milk and ¼ teaspoon vanilla in a small bowl; beat well. Drizzle over the coffee cake. Serve warm or at room temperature.

Serves 8

Chapter 7

Desserts

NewsChannel 5 has been a part of the
Children's Hospital Telethon since 1985.
Here, Angela and Harry Chapman with their children
Whit and Caroline in 1989.

NewsChannel 5

Elizabeth Owen keeps viewers informed with her "Consumer Alert" on NewsChannel 5. A culinary enthusiast, Elizabeth occassionally drops by **Talk of the Town** to prepare one of her favorite recipes.

NewsChannel 5 Morning Team: Beth Tucker and Joe Case.

Apple Dumplings

Lynne Tolley, Miss Mary Bobo's Boarding House

4   medium apples, peeled
¾   cup packed brown sugar
½   teaspoon salt
½   teaspoon cinnamon
    Grated peel of 1 lemon
¼   cup butter, softened
1   recipe (1-crust) pie pastry
1   egg white
1   tablespoon water
4   peaches or apricots, cut into halves
    Milk

▲ Core the apples and set aside. Mix the brown sugar, salt, cinnamon, lemon peel and butter in a small bowl. Spoon ⅔ of the mixture into the cored apples. Sprinkle the remaining mixture over the apples.

▲ Roll out the pie pastry to a ⅛-inch thickness. Cut into 4 squares. Beat the egg white and water in a small bowl. Brush the pastry squares with the beaten egg white. Place a peach half in the center of the square and top with an apple. Fold up the dough to enclose the fruit, sealing the edges with water. Prick with a fork in several places. Brush with milk. Place on a baking sheet.

▲ Bake at 450 degrees for 10 minutes. Reduce the oven temperature to 350 degrees. Bake for 45 minutes longer or until the apples are tender.

Serves 4

Miss Mary's Famous Baked Apricot Casserole

Lynne Tolley, Miss Mary Bobo's Boarding House

1   (17-ounce) can apricot halves, drained
1   cup packed light brown sugar
1½ cups butter cracker crumbs
½   cup butter

▲ Arrange the apricots cut-side down in a greased baking dish. Sprinkle with the brown sugar and the cracker crumbs. Dot with the butter.

▲ Bake at 325 degrees for 35 to 40 minutes or until the mixture is thickened and the top is crusty.

Serves 4 to 6

Bananas Foster

Michael Roussel, Brennan's Restaurant

4   bananas
¼   cup butter
1   cup packed brown sugar
½   teaspoon cinnamon
¼   cup banana liqueur
¼   cup rum
4   scoops vanilla ice cream

▲ Cut each banana into halves lengthwise. Cut each half into halves crosswise.

▲ Melt the butter in a flambé pan over medium heat. Add the brown sugar, cinnamon and banana liqueur, stirring to mix. Heat for several minutes.

▲ Add the bananas. Sauté for 1 to 2 minutes or until slightly softened and lightly browned. Add the rum. Cook for 30 seconds or until heated.

▲ Ignite the mixture with a match. Let flame until the alcohol is burned up and the flame subsides, tipping the pan with a circular motion to prolong the flaming.

▲ Place the ice cream into 4 serving bowls. Remove the bananas with a slotted spoon and arrange over the ice cream. Spoon the syrup from the pan over the bananas and ice cream. Serve immediately.

Serves 4

5 For a variation of Bananas Foster, try substituting Kahlúa for the banana liqueur, ¼ cup water for the rum and 1 tablespoon instant coffee granules for the cinnamon.

Banana Quesadillas with Rum Caramel Sauce

Debra Paquette, The Boun'dry

Vegetable oil for frying
12 (8-inch) flour tortillas
Banana Mixture
12 scoops cinnamon ice cream
Rum Caramel Sauce

▲ Heat the oil in a large skillet. Place a tortilla in the skillet. Spoon ½ to ¾ cup of the banana mixture over half of the tortilla; fold in half. Cook on each side until lightly browned. Repeat with the remaining tortillas.

▲ Place on serving plates. Top with a scoop of the ice cream. Drizzle with the Rum Caramel Sauce. May add chunked white chocolate or chocolate chips.

Banana Mixture

6 bananas, sliced
1 cup golden raisins
¾ cup packed brown sugar
Zest and juice of 1 lemon
⅓ cup dark rum
1 teaspoon cinnamon

▲ Combine the bananas, raisins, brown sugar, lemon zest and juice, rum and cinnamon in a saucepan.

▲ Cook over medium heat until thick and bubbly, stirring frequently. Remove from the heat and chill.

Rum Caramel Sauce

1 cup packed brown sugar
2 tablespoons instant coffee powder
3 to 4 ounces half-and-half
¼ cup butter
1 tablespoon corn syrup
2 ounces rum
½ to ¾ cup chopped pecans or walnuts

▲ Combine the brown sugar, coffee powder, half-and-half, butter and corn syrup in a saucepan.

▲ Cook over medium-high heat until the mixture begins to boil. Boil for 5 minutes, stirring constantly. Remove from the heat.

▲ Stir in the rum and pecans. Serve at room temperature or keep warm in a warm water bath.

Serves 12

Blackberry Cobbler

Mick's Restaurant

¾   cup sugar
¼   cup flour
     Dash of salt
2   pounds fresh blackberries, rinsed
1   tablespoon lemon juice
1   (9-inch) pie shell
½   cup flour
½   cup sugar
     Dash of cinnamon
¼   cup butter, softened

▲ Combine ¾ cup sugar, ¼ cup flour and salt in a medium bowl. Add the blackberries and lemon juice, tossing to coat. Spoon into the pie shell.

▲ Mix ½ cup flour, ½ cup sugar, cinnamon and butter in a small bowl, stirring until crumbly. Sprinkle over the blackberries.

▲ Bake at 325 degrees for 1 hour or until golden brown.

Serves 6 to 8

Blueberry Torte

Helma Ritter, Ole Heidelberg Restaurant

2   cups flour
½   cup packed brown sugar
1   cup melted butter
1½ cups chopped pecans or walnuts
6   ounces cream cheese, softened
1   cup confectioners' sugar
1   teaspoon vanilla extract
1   envelope whipped topping mix
1   (21-ounce) can blueberry pie filling

▲ Combine the flour, brown sugar, butter and pecans in a bowl; mix well. Pat the mixture over the bottom and up the sides of a 9x13-inch baking dish.

▲ Bake at 400 degrees for 15 minutes; cool.

▲ Cream the cream cheese, confectioners' sugar and vanilla in a mixer bowl until light and fluffy. Prepare the whipped topping using package instructions. Fold into the creamed mixture. Spread over the cooled crust; chill thoroughly.

▲ Spread the blueberry filling over the chilled mixture. Chill or serve at room temperature.

Serves 12

Fig Dessert with Mushroom Ice Cream

Bob Wagner, The Wild Boar

1 quart whipping cream

1 quart milk

4 medium cèpe mushrooms, finely chopped

10 egg yolks

1½ cups sugar

10 whole fresh figs, peeled

10 tablespoons butter

10 tablespoons sugar

▲ Combine the cream and milk in a large saucepan. Cook over medium-high heat until the mixture begins to boil, stirring constantly. Stir in the mushrooms; remove from the heat.

▲ Beat the egg yolks and sugar in a small bowl until thick and pale yellow. Beat a small amount of the cream mixture into the beaten egg yolks. Add the egg yolks gradually to the cream mixture, beating constantly.

▲ Cook over very low heat for 7 minutes, stirring constantly with a wooden spoon. Pour into the container of an ice cream freezer. Freeze using manufacturer's directions. Place in the freezer until ready to use.

▲ Cut halfway through the figs lengthwise. Place 1 tablespoon butter and 1 tablespoon sugar in each fig. Place on a baking sheet.

▲ Bake at 400 degrees for 10 minutes. Remove to serving plates. Top with the mushroom ice cream. Garnish with fresh berries.

Serves 10

5 For an easy refreshing dessert, shape scoops of lemon or orange sherbet into balls and roll in flaked coconut; freeze until firm. Serve over sliced strawberries or peaches.

Ginger-Poached Spiced Pears

Doc Holliday

1   cup water
1   cup orange juice
½   cup sugar
1   tablespoon grated fresh gingerroot
1   cinnamon stick
1   star anise, or ½ teaspoon anise seeds
4   medium pears
1   lemon, cut into halves

▲ Combine the water, orange juice, sugar, gingerroot, cinnamon and anise in a heavy medium saucepan. Bring to a boil; reduce heat. Simmer for 5 minutes, stirring frequently. Remove from the heat.

▲ Cut a thin slice from the bottom of each pear. Core from the bottom of the pear, leaving the stem intact. Peel and rub with the lemon. Place in the saucepan with the orange juice mixture. Squeeze the juice from the lemon over the pears and add the lemon halves to the mixture.

▲ Cook, covered, for 18 minutes or just until the pears are tender, turning occasionally. Remove and discard the lemons. Remove the pears with a slotted spoon to a bowl. Pour the liquid over the pears. Cover and chill thoroughly. May prepare to this point a day ahead.

▲ Remove the pears to individual serving plates, standing the pears upright. Pour the liquid into a heavy saucepan. Bring to a boil. Cook for 5 minutes or until the mixture thickens. Strain the syrup into a bowl. Cool in the freezer for 3 minutes. Spoon the syrup over the pears and serve.

Serves 4

Spirited Holiday Sugar Plums

Ann Clayton, Clayton-Blackmon

1   cup semisweet chocolate chips
¼   cup light corn syrup
½   cup sugar
⅓   cup brandy or whiskey
2½ cups finely ground vanilla wafers
1   cup finely chopped pecans
     Tinted sugar crystals
     Red and green candied cherry halves

▲ Melt the chocolate chips in the top of a double boiler over simmering water. Add the corn syrup, sugar, brandy, vanilla wafers and pecans, stirring until a thick paste forms. Remove from the heat.

▲ Shape the mixture into 1-inch balls. Roll in the tinted sugar. Top with a cherry half. Store in an airtight container. These improve with age.

Serves 48

TASTE OF **5** THE TOWN

Strawberry Flambé

Will Greenwood, Sunset Grill

1 pint strawberries, hulled
1 teaspoon butter
¼ cup packed brown sugar
¼ cup Grand Marnier

▲ Cut the strawberries into halves. Sauté in the butter in a medium saucepan until coated with butter. Add the brown sugar.

▲ Cook over medium heat until the strawberries are very soft. Remove from the heat. Add the Grand Marnier.

▲ Cook for 2 to 5 minutes or until the alcohol has burned off. Serve over ice cream or cake.

Serves 4 to 6

Strawberry Lasagna

Bill Monell, Monell's Dining and Catering

16 ounces cream cheese, softened
2 (3-ounce) packages vanilla instant pudding mix
½ cup confectioners' sugar
1 cup milk
8 cups mashed strawberries
¼ cup kirsch
1 cup sugar
2 loaves pound cake
1 cup whipping cream

▲ Beat the cream cheese, pudding mix, confectioners' sugar and milk in a mixer bowl at high speed until smooth.

▲ Combine the strawberries, kirsch and sugar in a medium bowl, mixing well. Remove 1 cup of the strawberry mixture. Purée in a food processor and reserve.

▲ Slice the pound cakes into ½-inch slices. Line a 9x13-inch dish with cake slices. Layer ⅓ of the cream cheese mixture, ⅓ of the strawberry mixture and half the remaining cake in the prepared dish. Layer half the remaining cream cheese mixture, half the remaining strawberry mixture, remaining cake and remaining cream cheese mixture in the prepared dish. Swirl the remaining strawberry mixture over the top. Chill for 4 to 8 hours.

▲ Whip the whipping cream in a small mixer bowl until stiff peaks form.

▲ Cut the dessert into 3-inch squares to serve. Top with the reserved strawberry purée and whipped cream.

Serves 10

Strawberries Romanoff

Nancy Crais, North Gate Inn, Monteagle, Tennessee

1   cup whipping cream
¼   cup confectioners' sugar
1   pint vanilla ice cream, softened
    Juice of 1 lemon
2   ounces Cointreau
1   ounce white rum
1   quart strawberries, hulled, chilled

▲ Whip the cream with the confectioners' sugar in a mixer bowl until stiff peaks form. Fold in the ice cream, lemon juice, Cointreau and rum.

▲ Spoon the strawberries into dessert dishes. Top with 3 to 4 tablespoons of the cream mixture.

Serves 8

Mary Ann's Famous Coconut Cream Pie

Dawn Wells, star of "Gilligan's Island"

3   egg yolks
    Dash of salt
3   cups milk
¾   cup sugar
2   tablespoons butter
½   cup cornstarch
1   cup flaked coconut
½   teaspoon vanilla extract
1   baked (9-inch) pie shell
3   egg whites
6   tablespoons (about) sugar
    Flaked coconut to taste

▲ Combine the egg yolks and salt in a double boiler. Beat over simmering water until blended. Stir in the milk, ¾ cup sugar and butter. Bring to a boil.

▲ Stir in a mixture of the cornstarch and a small amount of water gradually. Cook until thickened, whisking constantly. Stir in 1 cup coconut and vanilla. Spoon into the pie shell.

▲ Beat the egg whites in a mixer bowl until foamy. Add 6 tablespoons sugar gradually, beating constantly until stiff and glossy. Spread over the filling, sealing to the edge. Sprinkle with flaked coconut to taste.

▲ Bake at 400 degrees until light brown.

Serves 6

Angel Dessert

Natoma Riley

1   prepared angel food cake
2   small packages sugar-free vanilla instant pudding mix
4   cups skim milk
2½ pints fat-free sour cream
1   (21-ounce) can blueberry pie filling

▲ Break the cake into bite-sized pieces. Place in an 8x12-inch dish.

▲ Prepare the pudding mix with the milk using package directions. Fold in the sour cream. Pour over the cake layer. Top with the blueberry pie filling.

Serves 12

Grandmother Vavrusa's Buttermilk Kolache

Doc Holliday

12 ounces dried prunes
½   cup sugar
2¼ teaspoons cinnamon
1   cup water
2¼ cups flour
1   cup packed brown sugar
½   cup sugar
¾   cup vegetable oil
½   cup chopped walnuts
1   cup buttermilk
1   egg, beaten
1   teaspoon baking powder
1   teaspoon baking soda

▲ Cook the prunes, ½ cup sugar, ½ teaspoon of the cinnamon and water in a saucepan over medium heat until the prunes are soft. Mash with a fork and set aside to cool.

▲ Beat the flour, brown sugar, sugar, oil and ½ teaspoon of the cinnamon in a large bowl. Remove ¾ cup of the mixture to a medium bowl. Stir in the walnuts and 1¼ teaspoons cinnamon; set aside. Beat the buttermilk, egg, baking powder and baking soda in a small bowl. Add to the large bowl of the flour mixture, stirring until the batter is smooth.

▲ Pour the batter into a greased 9x12-inch baking pan. Spoon the prune mixture over the batter in 8 evenly spaced circles. Sprinkle with the walnut mixture, pressing into the batter with the back of a spoon.

▲ Bake at 350 degrees for 30 minutes or until firm and golden brown. Serve warm with unsalted butter.

Serves 8

Bread Pudding with Tennessee Whiskey Sauce

Lynne Tolley, Miss Mary Bobo's Boarding House

6 cups cubed French or Italian bread
1 cup raisins
1 apple, peeled, cored, grated
3 eggs
1 cup sugar
2 cups milk
1 teaspoon vanilla extract
$\frac{1}{2}$ teaspoon nutmeg
  Pinch of salt
  Tennessee Whiskey Sauce

▲ Combine the bread cubes, raisins and apple in a large bowl. Beat the eggs in a medium bowl until frothy; beat in the sugar. Add the milk, vanilla, nutmeg and salt, mixing well. Pour over the bread cubes. Let stand for 15 minutes.

▲ Spoon into a buttered 1$\frac{1}{2}$-quart baking dish. Place the baking dish in a larger pan filled with 1 inch of boiling water.

▲ Bake at 375 degrees for 40 to 45 minutes or until firm. Spoon onto serving plates and top with Tennessee Whiskey Sauce.

Tennessee Whiskey Sauce

1$\frac{1}{4}$ cups water
$\frac{1}{2}$ cup packed light brown sugar
$\frac{1}{4}$ teaspoon nutmeg
$\frac{1}{4}$ cup Jack Daniel's Whiskey
1$\frac{1}{2}$ tablespoons cornstarch
2 tablespoons butter

▲ Combine the water, brown sugar and nutmeg in a saucepan. Bring to a boil.

▲ Mix the whiskey and cornstarch in a small bowl until smooth. Stir into the brown sugar mixture.

▲ Cook until thickened, stirring frequently. Add the butter, stirring until melted.

Serves 8

Blueberry Mountain Cheesecake

JoAnna Lund, **Healthy Exchanges Cookbook**

16 ounces fat-free cream cheese, softened

1 small package sugar-free vanilla instant pudding mix

⅔ cup nonfat milk powder

1 cup Diet Mountain Dew

¾ cup light whipped topping

1½ teaspoons coconut extract

1 (6-ounce) Keebler butter-flavor pie shell

½ cup blueberry fruit spread

2 tablespoons flaked coconut

▲ Cream the cream cheese in a mixer bowl until light and fluffy. Add the pudding mix, milk powder and Mountain Dew. Whisk with a wire whisk until smooth. Fold in ¼ cup of the whipped topping and 1 teaspoon of the coconut extract.

▲ Spoon the mixture into the pie shell. Chill for 15 minutes or until set.

▲ Combine the blueberry spread, the remaining ½ teaspoon coconut extract and the remaining ½ cup whipped topping in a small bowl and mix well. Spread over the cheesecake. Sprinkle with the coconut.

▲ Chill until serving time.

Serves 6 to 8

 Create a quick dessert with fresh fruit slices, a dollop of sour cream or yogurt and a sprinkle of brown sugar or coconut.

Hazelnut Amaretto Chocolate Cheesecake

*A Friend of **Talk of the Town***

4 cups chocolate sandwich cookie crumbs

2 tablespoons cinnamon

¼ cup sugar

¼ cup melted butter

24 ounces cream cheese, softened

¾ cup sugar

4 eggs

1 cup sour cream

1 ounce amaretto liqueur

1 ounce hazelnut liqueur

8 ounces semisweet chocolate chips

¼ cup whipping cream

2 tablespoons butter

2 tablespoons vanilla extract

▲ Mix the cookie crumbs, cinnamon, ¼ cup sugar and melted butter in a small bowl. Press the mixture into a 9-inch pie plate; set aside.

▲ Cream the cream cheese, ¾ cup sugar and eggs in a mixer bowl until light and fluffy. Fold in the sour cream, amaretto and hazelnut liqueurs. Spoon into the prepared pie shell.

▲ Melt the chocolate chips with the cream in a saucepan over low heat, stirring constantly. Add the butter and vanilla. Cook until the butter is melted and the sauce thickens, stirring frequently. Remove from the heat. Pour over the cream cheese mixture.

▲ Bake at 300 degrees for 1½ hours.

Serves 6 to 8

 Use gingersnaps, chocolate wafers, vanilla wafers or sugar cookies to make a crumb pie shell.

Chess Squares

Donna McCabe, Loveless Cafe

6 tablespoons butter, softened
⅓ cup confectioners' sugar
1⅓ cups flour
½ cup butter, softened
1½ cups sugar
1 tablespoon yellow cornmeal
1 tablespoon vanilla extract
1 tablespoon distilled white vinegar
3 eggs, beaten

▲ Beat 6 tablespoons butter in a small mixer bowl until light and fluffy. Add the confectioners' sugar, beating to mix. Add the flour, beating until the mixture is crumbly. Press over the bottom of a 9-inch square baking pan.

▲ Beat ½ cup butter with sugar in a medium mixer bowl until the mixture is light and fluffy. Add the cornmeal, vanilla, vinegar and eggs, beating well. Pour into the prepared crust.

▲ Bake at 350 degrees for 20 to 25 minutes or until nearly set. Cool on a wire rack. Cut into squares to serve.

Serves 15

Chewy Caramel Brownies

*Holly Clegg, **Trim and Terrific American Favorites***

1 (9-ounce) package caramels
1 (14-ounce) can low-fat sweetened condensed milk
1 (2-layer) package light devil's food cake mix
½ cup melted light margarine
½ cup semisweet chocolate chips

▲ Melt the caramels with ⅓ cup of the condensed milk in the top of a double boiler over hot water, stirring frequently. Remove from heat and cover to keep warm.

▲ Combine the cake mix, melted margarine and the remaining condensed milk in a large mixer bowl. Beat at high speed until crumbly. Press half of the mixture over the bottom of a 9x13-inch baking pan sprayed with nonstick cooking spray and dusted with flour.

▲ Bake at 350 degrees for 6 minutes. Sprinkle with the chocolate chips. Spread the caramel mixture over the chocolate chips. Crumble the remaining chocolate cake mixture over the top.

▲ Bake for 15 minutes longer or until the brownies pull away from the side of the pan. Cool in the pan on a wire rack. Cut into squares to serve.

Serves 15

Pumpkin Cheesecake Bars

Ann Cox, Tennessee Egg and Poultry Association

1   (16-ounce) package pound cake mix

3   eggs

2   tablespoons melted butter or margarine

4   teaspoons pumpkin pie spice

8   ounces cream cheese, softened

1   (14-ounce) can sweetened condensed milk

1   (16-ounce) can pumpkin

½   teaspoon salt

1   cup chopped pecans or walnuts

▲ Combine the cake mix, 1 of the eggs, butter and 2 teaspoons of the pumpkin pie spice in a bowl, mixing until crumbly. Press over the bottom of a 10x15-inch baking pan.

▲ Beat the cream cheese in a mixer bowl until light and fluffy. Add the condensed milk, the remaining 2 eggs, the pumpkin, the remaining 2 teaspoons pumpkin pie spice and the salt, beating until smooth. Pour over the prepared crust. Sprinkle with the pecans.

▲ Bake at 350 degrees for 30 to 35 minutes or until firm. Chill in the refrigerator. Cut into bars to serve. Store in the refrigerator.

Serves 48

Pumpkin Squares

Lynne Tolley, Miss Mary Bobo's Boarding House

2   cups sugar

1   cup vegetable oil

4   eggs

2   cups flour

2   teaspoons baking soda

1   teaspoon baking powder

½   teaspoon salt

1   teaspoon nutmeg

2   teaspoons ground cinnamon

1   (16-ounce) can pumpkin

1   teaspoon vanilla extract

▲ Beat the sugar, oil and eggs in a large mixing bowl until light and fluffy.

▲ Sift the flour, baking soda, baking powder, salt, nutmeg and cinnamon together. Add to the egg mixture, mixing well. Stir in the pumpkin and vanilla. Pour into a 9x13-inch baking pan.

▲ Bake at 350 degrees for 25 to 35 minutes or until firm. Cut into squares to serve.

Serves 12 to 15

Surprise Packages

Ann Cox, Tennessee Egg and Poultry Association

8 ounces cream cheese, softened

1½ teaspoons salt

2⅓ cups sugar

3 eggs

1 cup semisweet chocolate chips

1 cup chopped pecans or walnuts

⅔ cup vegetable oil

3 cups flour

½ cup baking cocoa

2 teaspoons baking soda

2 cups buttermilk

2 teaspoons vanilla extract

▲ Cream the cream cheese, ½ teaspoon of the salt, ⅓ cup of the sugar and 1 of the eggs in a mixer bowl until light and fluffy. Fold in the chocolate chips and pecans; set aside.

▲ Beat the remaining 2 eggs with the oil in a large bowl. Combine the flour, the remaining sugar, baking cocoa, the remaining salt and baking soda in a bowl. Add to the egg mixture alternately with the buttermilk, beginning and ending with the flour mixture and beating well after each addition. Stir in the vanilla.

▲ Line muffin cups with paper liners. Fill ½ full with the batter. Spoon 1 tablespoon of the cream cheese mixture over the top.

▲ Bake at 350 degrees for 20 to 30 minutes or until the muffins test done. Batter will bake up over the filling, creating a surprise when tasted.

Serves 18

 Buy nuts in quantity and store them in airtight containers in the freezer. Frozen nuts are also easier to chop.

English Trifle

*Vicki Park, **Live! Don't Diet! Cookbook***

1   large package sugar-free vanilla instant pudding mix

4   cups skim milk

1   (2-layer) package yellow cake mix

½   cup fat-free egg substitute

1   (20-ounce) can light cherry pie filling

1   cup light nondairy whipped topping

▲ Prepare the pudding mix using skim milk. Chill until thickened.

▲ Prepare the cake using egg substitute. Bake using package directions for a 9x13-inch pan; cool. Slice into 1-inch thick slices.

▲ Layer the cake, pudding and pie filling in a clear dish, repeating layers until all ingredients have been used. Top with the whipped topping. May substitute fresh strawberries or blueberries for cherry pie filling.

Serves 12

Fantastic Trifle

*Holly Clegg, **Trim and Terrific American Favorites***

1   (16-ounce) angel food cake, cubed

⅔   cup sugar

3   tablespoons baking cocoa

1   tablespoon cornstarch

⅔   cup evaporated skim milk

¼   cup coffee liqueur

3   English toffee candy bars, crushed

3   (3-ounce) packages vanilla instant pudding mix

3   cups skim milk

2   bananas, peeled, sliced

12 ounces light whipped topping

▲ Arrange the cake cubes in a large bowl; set aside.

▲ Combine the sugar, cocoa, cornstarch and evaporated milk in a saucepan.

▲ Cook over low heat until the mixture thickens; remove from the heat. Stir in the coffee liqueur; cool. Pour over the cake cubes. Stir in the crushed toffee bars.

▲ Beat the pudding mix with the skim milk in a mixer bowl until thickened. Pour over the cake mixture. Chill for 15 minutes.

▲ Layer the cake mixture, bananas and whipped topping ½ at a time in a large glass trifle bowl, ending with the whipped topping.

Serves 16

Tiger Butter

Halley Neal, Granny's Gourmet

1 pound white chocolate, coarsely chopped
12 ounces peanut butter
2 cups semisweet chocolate chips

▲ Combine the white chocolate and peanut butter in a heavy saucepan. Cook over low heat until the white chocolate is melted, stirring constantly.

▲ Heat the chocolate chips in a small heavy saucepan until melted, stirring frequently.

▲ Spread the white chocolate evenly on a waxed-paper-lined 10x15-inch jelly roll pan. Drizzle the chocolate over the surface and swirl with a knife. Chill until firm. Cut into pieces. Store in a covered container in the refrigerator.

Serves 72

Low-Fat Carrot Cake

Jack Favier, Baptist Hospital Executive Chef

1 cup sugar
1½ cups pastry flour
1 tablespoon baking soda
1 teaspoon salt
2 teaspoons cinnamon
1 teaspoon baking powder
½ cup applesauce
2 eggs
1 cup carrot purée
6 ounces cream cheese, softened
6 red cherry halves

▲ Combine the sugar, flour, baking soda, salt, cinnamon, baking powder and applesauce in a large bowl; stir until smooth. Add the eggs 1 at a time, beating well after each addition. Stir in the carrot purée. Pour into a floured 9-inch cake pan.

▲ Bake at 350 degrees for 35 to 40 minutes or until the cake tests done. Cool in the pan for 5 minutes; turn onto a wire rack to cool completely.

▲ Beat the cream cheese in a mixer bowl until light and fluffy. Spread over the cooled cake. Top with the cherry halves.

Serves 8

Fresh Coconut Cake

Lynne Tolley, Miss Mary Bobo's Boarding House

I	fresh coconut
I	cup butter, softened
2	cups sugar
8	egg whites
I	teaspoon vanilla extract
¼	teaspoon almond extract
I	cup milk
3¼	cups flour
4	teaspoons baking powder
¼	teaspoon salt
⅓	cup confectioners' sugar
	Vanilla Frosting

▲ Pierce the 3 eyes of the coconut with an ice pick or skewer. Drain and reserve the liquid. Bake the coconut at 400 degrees for 15 minutes or until the hard shell cracks. Split the coconut into halves and cut out the coconut meat. Peel off any brown membrane. Grate the coconut and reserve.

▲ Cream the butter and sugar in a mixer bowl until light and fluffy. Add the egg whites, beating well. Stir in the vanilla and almond extracts. Add ½ cup of the milk, beating well.

▲ Sift the flour, baking powder and salt together. Add to the creamed mixture alternately with the remaining milk, beating well after each addition. Pour into 2 greased and floured 9-inch cake pans.

▲ Bake at 350 degrees for 45 minutes or until the layers test done. Transfer to a wire rack to cool completely. Split the cooled layers into halves horizontally.

▲ Mix the reserved coconut liquid and the confectioners' sugar in a small bowl. Sprinkle evenly over the top of each layer. Spread the Vanilla Frosting over each layer and sprinkle with fresh coconut. Stack the layers and spread the frosting over the top and side of the cake. Sprinkle with the remaining coconut. Let stand for 10 minutes before cutting.

Vanilla Frosting

2	cups sugar
2	tablespoons light corn syrup
⅔	cup water
2	egg whites, stiffly beaten
2	teaspoons vanilla extract
½	teaspoon almond extract

▲ Combine the sugar, corn syrup and water in a saucepan. Bring to a boil. Cook until the sugar dissolves, stirring constantly; remove from the heat.

▲ Add ⅓ cup of the hot syrup gradually to the stiffly beaten egg whites, beating constantly. Cook the remaining syrup over medium-high heat until a candy thermometer registers 238 to 240 degrees, soft-ball stage; do not stir.

▲ Add the hot syrup to the egg whites, beating at high speed. Add the vanilla and almond extracts, beating continuously for 5 minutes or until the frosting is of spreading consistency.

Serves 12 to 15

TASTE OF **5** THE TOWN

The Fruitcake Hater's Fruitcake

Betty Rosbottom

3 large navel oranges
1 cup dried cranberries
¾ cup golden raisins
½ cup currants
½ cup chopped dried apricots
2 cups sugar
1 cup butter, softened
4 eggs
1 teaspoon vanilla extract
3 cups flour
1 teaspoon baking soda
½ teaspoon ground cinnamon
¼ teaspoon ground ginger
¼ teaspoon ground nutmeg
1 cup buttermilk
1 cup chopped walnuts
8 ounces cream cheese, softened
6 tablespoons confectioners' sugar

▲ Grate the peel of the oranges, reserving 3 tablespoons for the cake and 2 teaspoons for the frosting. Squeeze the juice from the oranges, reserving ⅔ cup juice for the cake and ¼ cup for the frosting.

▲ Combine the cranberries, raisins, currants, apricots and the reserved ⅔ cup orange juice in a saucepan. Bring to a boil; reduce the heat. Simmer for 5 minutes or until the fruit is plumped. Drain and set aside.

▲ Cream the sugar and the butter in a large mixer bowl until light and fluffy. Add the eggs 1 at a time, beating well after each addition. Stir in the reserved 3 tablespoons orange peel and the vanilla.

▲ Combine the flour, baking soda, cinnamon, ginger and nutmeg in a bowl. Add to the creamed mixture alternately with the buttermilk, beating well after each addition and beginning and ending with the flour mixture. Fold in the walnuts and the plumped fruit. Pour into a buttered and floured 10-inch tube pan.

▲ Bake at 325 degrees for 1¼ hours or until the cake tests done. Cool in the pan for 10 minutes. Remove to a wire rack to cool completely.

▲ Beat the cream cheese and confectioners' sugar in a mixer bowl until light and fluffy. Add the reserved ¼ cup orange juice and 2 teaspoons orange zest, beating until smooth. Spread over the cooled cake. Garnish with additional dried fruit.

▲ May store, covered, in the refrigerator for 5 days. Let stand at room temperature for 30 minutes before serving. May freeze, wrapped tightly in heavy-duty foil, for up to 2 months. Defrost in the refrigerator and let stand at room temperature for 30 minutes before serving.

Serves 12 to 15

Bulla's Fudge Cake with Fudge Frosting

*Daisy King, **Miss Daisy Celebrates Tennessee***

4 ounces unsweetened baking chocolate

2 cups sugar

1 cup butter, softened

4 eggs

2 cups minus 2 tablespoons flour

1 cup chopped pecans

2 teaspoons vanilla extract

Fudge Frosting

▲ Melt the chocolate in the top of a double boiler over hot water, stirring frequently; remove from the heat and set aside.

▲ Cream the sugar and butter in a mixer bowl until light and fluffy. Stir in the melted chocolate. Add the eggs 1 at a time, beating well after each addition. Stir in the flour gradually. Fold in the pecans and vanilla. Pour into two nonstick 8-inch square cake pans.

▲ Bake at 325 degrees for 25 minutes. Cool in the pans for 5 minutes. Remove to wire racks.

▲ Spread the Fudge Frosting between the layers and over the top and side of the cake while still warm. Let stand for several minutes before serving.

Fudge Frosting

2 cups sugar

⅔ cup milk

¼ teaspoon salt

2 ounces unsweetened baking chocolate

½ cup shortening or butter

2 teaspoons vanilla extract

▲ Combine the sugar, milk, salt, chocolate and shortening in a heavy saucepan.

▲ Cook over low heat until the mixture begins to boil and the sugar dissolves, stirring constantly. Boil for 3 minutes longer but do not stir; remove from the heat. Let stand to cool for several minutes.

▲ Add the vanilla, beating until of spreading consistency. May add a few drops of cream to thin slightly.

Serves 8 to 10

Fresh Lemon Sunshine Cake

Marie Rama, "The Lemon Lady"

6 egg whites, at room temperature

½ teaspoon cream of tartar

1½ cups sugar

6 egg yolks

3 tablespoons fresh lemon juice

5 tablespoons water
   Grated peel of 1 lemon

1½ cups sifted cake flour

¼ teaspoon salt

1½ cups sifted confectioners' sugar

1½ to 2 tablespoons freshly squeezed
   lemon juice

▲ Beat the egg whites in a large mixer bowl until foamy. Add the cream of tartar, beating until soft peaks form. Add ½ cup of the sugar 2 tablespoons at a time, beating until stiff peaks form; set aside.

▲ Beat the egg yolks in a mixer bowl for 2 minutes or until thick and pale yellow. Add the remaining 1 cup sugar gradually, beating at high speed until the mixture is thick and the sugar is dissolved. Add 3 tablespoons lemon juice and water, beating until smooth. Stir in the lemon peel.

▲ Sift the flour and the salt together. Add to the egg yolk mixture, stirring until smooth. Fold the mixture into the beaten egg whites. Pour into an ungreased 10-inch tube pan. Cut through the batter with a knife to remove air bubbles.

▲ Bake at 325 degrees for 1 hour or until the cake tests done. Invert the pan onto a wire rack and let stand for 1½ hours to cool. Loosen the cake from the pan with a narrow spatula. Invert onto a cake plate.

▲ Beat the confectioners' sugar with 1½ tablespoons lemon juice until smooth, adding additional lemon juice for desired consistency. Spread over the top of the cooled cake, allowing some of the glaze to drizzle over the edge.

Serves 12 to 15

Light Red Velvet Cake

Natoma Riley

½ cup fat-free low-calorie margarine, softened

4 ounces fat-free cream cheese, softened

1½ cups sugar

½ cup egg substitute

2 (1-ounce) bottles red food coloring

2¼ cups sifted cake flour

2 tablespoons unsweetened baking cocoa

1 teaspoon baking soda

¼ teaspoon salt

1 cup low-fat buttermilk

1 teaspoon vanilla extract

Boiled Frosting

▲ Beat the margarine and cream cheese in a mixer bowl at medium speed until light and fluffy. Add the sugar gradually, beating well after each addition. Stir in the egg substitute and food coloring, beating well.

▲ Combine the flour, baking cocoa, baking soda and salt in a bowl. Add to the creamed mixture alternately with the buttermilk, beating well after each addition. Stir in the vanilla. Pour into three 9-inch cake pans sprayed with nonstick cooking spray.

▲ Bake at 350 degrees for 18 minutes. Cool in the pans on a wire rack for 10 minutes. Remove the cakes to a wire rack and cool completely.

▲ Spread the Boiled Frosting between the layers and over the top and side of the cake.

Boiled Frosting

1½ cups sugar

¾ cup water

1 tablespoon light corn syrup

2 egg whites

⅛ teaspoon salt

1 teaspoon vanilla extract

▲ Reserve 2 tablespoons of the sugar. Combine the remaining sugar, water and corn syrup in a heavy saucepan.

▲ Cook over medium heat until the sugar dissolves and the syrup is clear, stirring constantly. Cook without stirring until a candy thermometer registers 240 degrees (soft-ball stage). Remove from the heat.

▲ Beat the egg whites and salt until soft peaks form. Beat in the reserved sugar gradually. Add the syrup mixture gradually, beating constantly. Add the vanilla, beating until stiff peaks form and the frosting is thick.

Serves 16

Holiday Banana Nog Pie

*JoAnna Lund, **Healthy Exchanges Cookbook***

2   bananas, chopped
1   (6-ounce) Keebler butter-flavor
     pie shell
1   small package sugar-free vanilla
     instant pudding mix
⅔   cup nonfat dry milk powder
1¼   cups water
¾   cup low-fat whipped topping
1   teaspoon rum extract
¼   teaspoon ground nutmeg

▲ Spread the bananas in the pie shell; set aside.

▲ Combine the pudding mix, milk powder and water in a bowl. Mix with a wire whisk until smooth. Fold in ¼ cup of the whipped topping, the rum extract and nutmeg. Spread evenly over the bananas.

▲ Chill for 10 minutes. Spread the remaining ½ cup whipped topping over the pie. Garnish with additional nutmeg. Chill for 2 hours before serving.

Serves 6 to 8

South Seas Chocolate Tarts

*JoAnna Lund, **Healthy Exchanges Cookbook***

2   cups sliced bananas
6   Keebler single-serve graham
     cracker tart shells
1   small package sugar-free chocolate
     instant pudding mix
⅔   cup nonfat dry milk powder
1½   cups water
¼   teaspoon coconut extract
6   tablespoons light whipped topping
2   teaspoons flaked coconut

▲ Place an equal portion of the bananas into each tart shell; set aside.

▲ Combine the pudding mix, milk powder, water and coconut extract in a bowl. Mix with a wire whisk until smooth. Spoon evenly over the bananas.

▲ Combine the whipped topping and coconut in a small bowl. Spoon onto each tart. Chill for 1 hour before serving.

Serves 6

Doug Darling's Makes-Its-Own-Crust Coconut Pie

Jim Clark, **Aunt Bee's Delightful Desserts**

4 eggs

2 cups milk

1¾ cups sugar

1½ cups flaked coconut

½ cup flour

1 teaspoon vanilla extract

¼ cup melted margarine

▲ Beat the eggs and milk in a large bowl. Add the sugar, coconut, flour, vanilla and margarine, mixing well. Pour into a greased 10-inch pie plate.

▲ Bake at 350 degrees for 45 minutes or until golden brown. The pie should have a delicate crust on the top, side and bottom. Cool before serving.

Serves 8

Fruit Tart

Daniel Bourgeois, Opryland Hotel

9 ounces unsalted butter, softened

4½ ounces confectioners' sugar

2 eggs, beaten

18 ounces flour

Dash of baking powder

½ quart milk

4½ ounces sugar

4 egg yolks

¼ cup flour

2 cups chopped fresh fruit

▲ Cream the butter and confectioners' sugar in a bowl. Add the eggs, beating well. Sift 18 ounces flour and baking powder together. Add to the creamed mixture.

▲ Knead to form a soft dough. Let rise for 15 minutes in the refrigerator. Roll out to a ¼-inch-thick circle. Place in a 9-inch tart pan.

▲ Bake at 400 degrees for 20 minutes. Let cool.

▲ Combine the milk with ½ of the sugar in a saucepan. Bring to a boil; remove from the heat.

▲ Combine the egg yolks with the remaining sugar in a bowl, mixing well. Sift ¼ cup flour into the egg mixture, whisking until mixed. Pour ¼ of the milk mixture gradually into the egg yolk mixture, stirring constantly. Pour into the saucepan with the remaining milk mixture.

▲ Heat for 15 to 20 seconds, stirring constantly. Pour into a bowl and let stand to cool. Beat until smooth. Spread over the cooled pastry crust. Top with the fresh fruit. Garnish with fruit glaze.

Serves 6

Heath Bar Cake

Vada Thomas, Potluck Contest Winner

½ teaspoon salt

1½ cups sugar

¾ cup packed brown sugar

3 cups flour

¾ cup butter or margarine

2 eggs

1½ teaspoons vanilla extract

1½ cups buttermilk

1½ teaspoons baking soda

½ cup chopped nuts

5 Heath Bars, broken

▲ Combine the salt, sugar, brown sugar and flour in a bowl; mix well. Reserve ½ cup of the mixture.

▲ Add the butter, eggs, vanilla, buttermilk and baking soda to the remaining mixture and mix well. Pour into a greased and floured 9x13-inch cake pan.

▲ Add nuts and Heath Bars to the reserved mixture; sprinkle over the top of the cake.

▲ Bake at 350 degrees for 30 minutes or until the cake tests done.

Serves 8 to 10

 An apple cut in half and placed in the cake container will keep the cake fresh for several days longer.

D'Liteful Pumpkin Pie

Lisa Sheehan-Smith, Baptist Hospital

2   cups gingersnap cookie crumbs
5   tablespoons melted margarine
8   ounces fat-free cream cheese,
    softened
1   (14-ounce) can low-fat sweetened
    condensed milk
1   (16-ounce) can solid-pack pumpkin
2   teaspoons pumpkin pie spice
¼   teaspoon salt
1   teaspoon vanilla extract
½   cup egg substitute

▲ Combine the cookie crumbs and margarine in a small bowl, tossing well. Press the mixture over the bottom of a 9-inch pie plate sprayed with nonstick cooking spray.

▲ Cream the cream cheese in a mixer bowl at medium speed until light and fluffy. Add the condensed milk gradually, beating constantly until smooth. Add the pumpkin, spice, salt and vanilla, mixing well. Stir in the egg substitute. Pour into the prepared pie plate.

▲ Bake at 350 degrees for 40 minutes or until the pie is set. Cool on a wire rack for 40 minutes. Chill in the refrigerator for 2 hours before serving.

Serves 6 to 8

Raspberry Pie

Tammy Algood, Tennessee Agricultural Extension Service

1½ cups water
1½ cups sugar
2   drops of red food coloring
3   tablespoons cornstarch
3   tablespoons raspberry gelatin
4   cups raspberries
1   baked (9-inch) pie shell

▲ Combine the water, sugar, food coloring, cornstarch and raspberry gelatin in a saucepan.

▲ Cook over medium heat until the sugar and gelatin are dissolved; remove from the heat. Let stand to cool. Fold in the raspberries. Pour into the pie shell.

▲ Chill in the refrigerator before serving.

Serves 6 to 8

Gingersnaps

Doc Holliday

1½ cups packed brown sugar

¼ cup blackstrap or dark molasses

1 egg, at room temperature

1 cup melted butter, cooled

4¾ cups sifted flour

2 teaspoons ground ginger

1½ teaspoons ground cloves

1½ teaspoons ground cinnamon

1½ teaspoons baking soda

⅜ teaspoon salt

Sugar

▲ Combine the brown sugar, molasses and egg in a large bowl; mix well.

▲ Beat in the butter. Stir in the flour, ginger, cloves, cinnamon, baking soda and salt.

▲ Turn out onto a lightly floured surface. Shape into 4 long logs and roll until firm. Cut each log into halves crosswise. Roll each half to a ⅝-inch diameter.

▲ Freeze for 1 hour.

▲ Pour sugar into a shallow bowl to a ¼-inch depth. Cut the logs into ¼-inch slices. Dip the slices in the sugar, turning to coat. Press to a ⅛-inch thickness. Place the slices about 1 inch apart on a greased nonstick cookie sheet.

▲ Bake at 350 degrees for 6 to 8 minutes or until lightly browned but still soft. Cool on the cookie sheet for 30 seconds or just until set. Remove immediately with a spatula to a sheet of waxed paper. Sprinkle with sugar.

▲ May store in an airtight container in a cool place for up to 1 month.

Serves 40 to 50

5 Every drop of molasses or honey will come out of the measuring cup if it is first rubbed with margarine.

Peanut Butter Popcorn Balls

Gerry Failla

½ cup unpopped corn
2 tablespoons melted butter
  Salt to taste
⅔ cup white corn syrup
1 cup packed brown sugar
1 cup peanut butter

▲ Pop corn. Place in a large bowl. Season with butter and salt. Remove all unpopped kernels. Mix corn syrup and brown sugar together in a small saucepan.

▲ Cook over medium heat until bubbly, stirring constantly. Add peanut butter. Cook over low heat until mixed well. Pour over popcorn evenly. Mix well with spoon.

▲ Pour onto cookie sheet. Let cool for 5 minutes. Shape into balls quickly with buttered hands.

Yields 15 servings

Chocolate Decadent Cookies

Pat Robinson, Front Porch Cafe

3½ cups semisweet chocolate chips

4   ounces bittersweet chocolate

6   tablespoons butter

⅓   cup flour

¼   teaspoon baking powder

¼   teaspoon salt

3   eggs

1   cup sugar

2   teaspoons vanilla extract

1   cup pecans (optional)

1   cup walnuts (optional)

▲ Combine 2 cups of the chocolate chips and the bittersweet chocolate with the butter in a microwave-safe bowl. Microwave for 2½ minutes. Stir until smooth; cool.

▲ Sift the flour, baking powder and salt together.

▲ Beat the eggs, sugar and vanilla in a mixer bowl until light and fluffy. Add the cooled chocolate and the flour mixture, beating well. Fold in the remaining chocolate chips, pecans and walnuts. Drop by teaspoonfuls onto a lightly greased cookie sheet.

▲ Bake at 350 degrees for 6 to 8 minutes or until cracks form on top. Do not overbake.

Serves 36

Chocolate Truffles

Scott Thurman, Regal Maxwell House Hotel

1   cup heavy cream

1   tablespoon instant coffee powder

1   ounce Kahlúa

1   pound semisweet chocolate chips

▲ Bring the cream to a scant boil in a heavy saucepan; remove from the heat. Stir in the coffee powder and the Kahlúa. Pour the mixture into a bowl. Add the chocolate chips, stirring until smooth. Chill, covered, for 8 hours to overnight.

▲ Shape the mixture into balls. Place on a tray; chill for several hours. Dip in melted chocolate, confectioners' sugar, shaved chocolate or cocoa powder to garnish.

Serves 24 to 30

Index

ACCOMPANIMENTS. *See also* Salsa
Key Lime Mustard Sauce, 126
Maple Walnut Butter, 112
Mustard Sauce, 124
Pepper Jelly, 108
Red Sauce, 123
Roasted Garlic Alfredo
Sauce, 131
Wild Mushroom Sauce, 115

APPETIZERS
Baked Artichoke Dip, 33
Baked Brie with Apple Chutney, 36
Black Bean Layered Dip, 33
Cheesy Mexican Dip, 34
Chile Crab Egg Roll, 37
Chunky Vegetable Dip, 35
Doc Holliday's Special Hot Mushroom
Dip, 35
Easy Cheese Canapés, 36
Fried Crab Won Tons, 37
Greek Pastries, 38
Stuffed Grape Leaves [Dolmades], 11
Tortilla Bites, 38

APPLE
Apple Dumplings, 157
Apples with Cranberries, 22
Baked Brie with Apple Chutney, 36
Chicken with Brie and Apples, 90

BANANA
Banana Quesadillas with Rum
Caramel Sauce, 159
Bananas Foster, 158
Fat-Free Fruit Salad, 55
Holiday Banana Nog Pie, 179
Pan Salad, 14

BEANS. *See also* Black Beans
Baked Bean Combo, 71
Bean-Stuffed Cabbage
Rolls, 72
Chicken and White Bean Stew with
Cilantro and Basil, 47
Corky's Fifteen-Bean Soup, 41
Country-Style Sautéed Green
Beans, 74
Lima Bean Risotto, 75
Nancy and George Jones' Favorite
Soup, 43
Roasted Tomato and White Bean
Soup, 42

BEEF. *See also* Ground Beef
Beef and Sausage Shish Kabobs, 106
Beef with Oyster Sauce, 100
Crescent-Topped Beef Potpie, 101
Hungarian Goulash, 103
Sportsman's Casserole, 18
Steak and Chicken Fajitas, 95
Tennessee Tenderloin Tips, 104
Yakiniku Donburi [Fried Beef and
Vegetables on Rice], 102

BEVERAGES
Boiled Custard, 31
Buttermilk Blast, 29
Cinnamon Coffee, 30
International Coffees, 30
Light Holiday Eggnog, 31
Lyric Springs Lemonade, 32
Mocha Coffee, 30
Orange Coffee, 30
Peanut Butter and Jelly Punch, 32
Skinny Coffee Milkshake, 29
Strawberry Smoothie, 29

BISCUITS
Potato Dill Biscuits, 146
Sweet Potato Biscuits, 147

BLACK BEANS
Black Bean Chili with Beer and
Chipotle Peppers, 45
Black Bean Layered Dip, 33
Southwest Salad, 68
Thirty-Minute Beef and Black Bean
Soup, 41
Tortilla Bites, 38

Blackening Spice, 128

BLUEBERRY
Angel Dessert, 165
Berry Cool Summer Salad, 55
Blueberry Mountain Cheesecake, 167
Blueberry Peach Cake, 24
Blueberry Torte, 160

BREADS. *See also* Biscuits; Coffee
Cakes; Muffins; Rolls
Apricot-Coconut Bread, 141
Bacon Cheese Bread, 143
Carrot Nut Pancakes, 151
Chocolate Zucchini Bread, 142
Coconut Crescents, 147

Farm Pumpkin Bread, 144
Healthier Version of Joe Case's Killer
Kornbread, 149
Pumpkin Bread Roll, 144
Sour Cream Cherry Walnut
Bread, 145

CAKES
Aunt Lulu's White Butter Cake, 25
Bulla's Fudge Cake with Fudge
Frosting, 176
Fresh Coconut Cake, 174
Fresh Lemon Sunshine Cake, 177
Heath Bar Cake, 181
Light Red Velvet Cake, 178
Low-Fat Carrot Cake, 173
My Boys' Favorite Lemon Cake, 25
The Fruitcake Hater's Fruitcake, 175

CANDY
Chocolate Truffles, 185
Lelan's Fudge, 26
Peanut Butter Popcorn Balls, 184
Spirited Holiday Sugar Plums, 162
Tiger Butter, 173

CARROTS
Carrot Nut Pancakes, 151
Cream of Carrot Soup, 44
Low-Fat Carrot Cake, 173

CHEESECAKES
Blueberry Mountain Cheesecake, 167
Cheesecake, 22
Hazelnut Amaretto Chocolate
Cheesecake, 168

CHICKEN
Caesar's Symphony Soup, 53
Chicken and White Bean Stew with
Cilantro and Basil, 47
Chicken with Brie and Apples, 90
Chipotle Chicken with Mango and
Cranberries, 91
Crispy Fried Chicken, 89
Curried Shrimp and Chicken, 121
Deep South Chicken Stew, 44
Grilled Ginger Chicken, 92
Louisiana Gumbo, 49
Minnie Pearl's Chicken Tetrazzini, 98
Mother and Child Chicken, 92
New Orleans-Style Chicken, 93
Pasta Yaya, 135

TASTE OF **5** THE TOWN

Index

Picnic Herbed Chicken, 87
Puffy Chicken Chiles Rellenos, 97
Rasta Pasta, 128
Roast Chicken with Herbs and White Wine, 88
St. Patrick's Day Pasta, 136
Sautéed Chicken with Mediterranean Vegetables, 94
Smoked Chicken Pasta Pie with Roasted Garlic Alfredo Sauce, 131
Spicy Ginger Chicken, 96
Steak and Chicken Fajitas, 95
Swett's Famous Southern Fried Chicken, 89

CHILI
Barb Wire's Real Texas-Style Chili, 46
Black Bean Chili with Beer and Chipotle Peppers, 45
Christmas Chili, 12
Sunset Grill Basic Chili, 45
Vegetarian Chili, 13

CHOCOLATE
Bulla's Fudge Cake with Fudge Frosting, 176
Chewy Caramel Brownies, 169
Chocolate Decadent Cookies, 185
Chocolate-Filled Snowballs, 24
Chocolate Truffles, 185
Chocolate Zucchini Bread, 142
Fudge Frosting, 176
Fudge Pie, 23
Lelan's Fudge, 26
Light Red Velvet Cake, 178
Peanut Butter and Jelly Punch, 32
South Seas Chocolate Tarts, 179
Surprise Packages, 171
Tiger Butter, 173

COCONUT
Apricot-Coconut Bread, 141
Coconut Crescents, 147
Doug Darling's Makes-Its-Own-Crust Coconut Pie, 180
Fresh Coconut Cake, 174
Mary Ann's Famous Coconut Cream Pie, 164

COFFEE CAKES
After the Opry Coffee Cake, 152
Quick and Easy Coffee Cake, 153

Raspberry-Almond Coffee Cake, 154
Raspberry Coffee Cake, 153

COOKIES
Chess Squares, 169
Chewy Caramel Brownies, 169
Chocolate Decadent Cookies, 185
Chocolate-Filled Snowballs, 24
Gingersnaps, 183
Pumpkin Cheesecake Bars, 170
Pumpkin Squares, 170

CORN
Chilled Corn Chowder, 47
Corn Pudding, 73
Healthier Version of Joe Case's Killer Kornbread, 149
Layered Corn Bread Salad, 59
Quick Corn Relish, 84
Shoe Peg Corn Casserole, 73

CRAB MEAT
Al's Shrimp and Crab Pasta Salad, 65
Ann's Crab Cakes with Mustard Sauce, 124
Cannellini and Crab Meat Soup, 43
Chile Crab Egg Roll, 37
Fried Crab Won Tons, 37
Maryland Crab Cakes, 125

DESSERTS. See also Cakes; Candy; Cookies; Pies; Tarts
Angel Dessert, 165
Apple Dumplings, 157
Apples with Cranberries, 22
Banana Quesadillas with Rum Caramel Sauce, 159
Bananas Foster, 158
Blackberry Cobbler, 160
Blueberry Mountain Cheesecake, 167
Blueberry Peach Cake, 24
Blueberry Torte, 160
Bread Pudding with Tennessee Whiskey Sauce, 166
Cheesecake, 22
English Trifle, 172
Fantastic Trifle, 172
Fig Dessert with Mushroom Ice Cream, 161
Ginger-Poached Spiced Pears, 162
Grandmother Vavrusa's Buttermilk Kolache, 165

Hazelnut Amaretto Chocolate Cheesecake, 168
Miss Mary's Famous Baked Apricot Casserole, 157
Momma Case's Biscuit Puddin', 23
Strawberries Romanoff, 164
Strawberry Flambé, 163
Strawberry Lasagna, 163
Surprise Packages, 171

DESSERTS, SAUCES
Rum Caramel Sauce, 159
Tennessee Whiskey Sauce, 166

DIPS
Baked Artichoke Dip, 33
Black Bean Layered Dip, 33
Cheesy Mexican Dip, 34
Chunky Vegetable Dip, 35
Doc Holliday's Special Hot Mushroom Dip, 35

DUCK
Duck and Warm Brie Salad, 62

EGG DISHES
Eggs Fiesta, 16
Mexican Strata, 34

FISH
Baked Salmon with Papaya Salsa, 118
Baked Tilapia, 117
Broiled Orange Roughy, 116
Caraway-Crusted Grilled Salmon with Pineapple and Green Tomato Salsa, 119
Caribbean Seafood Stew, 51
Caribbean Smoked Fish Pie, 117
Cedar-Planked Salmon, 120
Oven-Fried Catfish, 116
Seafood Basil Pasta à la Hummell, 127
Trout with Lemon Dill Sauce, 120

FROSTINGS
Boiled Frosting, 178
Fudge Frosting, 176
Vanilla Frosting, 174

GAME
Sure-Shot Rabbit, 114
Vension Chops, Country Ham and Wild Mushroom Sauce, 115

Index

GROUND BEEF
Barb Wire's Real Texas-Style Chili, 46
Black-Eyed Pea Pasta, 130
Cabbage Casserole, 71
Christmas Chili, 12
Hopping John 17
Mark's "Lasagna of Love," 18
Stuffed Grape Leaves
    [Dolmades], 11
Sunset Grill Basic Chili, 45
Thirty-Minute Beef and Black Bean
    Soup, 41
Twenty-Minute Tamale Pie, 105
Upside-Down Pizza, 107

GUMBO
Crawfish Gumbo, 48
Louisiana Gumbo, 49

HAM
Country Ham, 110
Pesto, Prawns, Prosciutto and
    Pasta, 127
Vension Chops, Country Ham and
    Wild Mushroom Sauce, 115

LAMB
Boneless Leg of Lamb, 107
Mid-Eastern Skillet Dinner, 109
Roasted Rack of Lamb with Pepper
    Jelly and Mashed Potatoes, 108

LEMON
Fresh Lemon Sunshine Cake, 177
Lyric Springs Lemonade, 32
My Boys' Favorite Lemon Cake, 25
Trout with Lemon Dill Sauce, 120

MUFFINS
Potato Parmesan Muffins, 149
Spiced Whole Wheat Muffins, 150

ONIONS
Baked Vidalia Onions, 76
Family Reunion Onion Casserole, 76

PASTA. *See also* Salads, Pasta
Angel Hair Pomodoro, 21
Black-Eyed Pea Pasta, 130
Caesar's Symphony Soup, 53
Fettuccini "What's To Cook
    Tonight," 132

Italian Non-Meatballs, 138
Mark's "Lasagna of Love," 18
Mediterranean Pasta, 133
Minnie Pearl's Chicken
    Tetrazzini, 98
Pasta Feta Delight, 134
Pasta-Vegetable Soup, 12
Pasta Yaya, 135
Pesto, Prawns, Prosciutto and
    Pasta, 127
Rasta Pasta, 128
St. Patrick's Day Pasta, 136
Sautéed Broccoli Spaghetti, 132
Seafood Basil Pasta à la
    Hummell, 127
Shrimp Stroganoff, 20
Smoked Chicken Pasta Pie with
    Roasted Garlic Alfredo
    Sauce, 131
Spaghetti Al Picchi Pacchio, 129
Spinach Lasagna, 137

PEACH
Blueberry Peach Cake, 24
Fat-Free Fruit Salad, 55
Fresh Fruit Salad, 56

PIES
D'Liteful Pumpkin Pie, 182
Doug Darling's Makes-Its-Own-Crust
    Coconut Pie, 180
Fudge Pie, 23
Holiday Banana Nog Pie, 179
Mary Ann's Famous Coconut Cream
    Pie, 164
Raspberry Pie, 182

PORK. *See also* Ham; Sausage
Eggs Fiesta, 16
Hungarian Goulash, 103
Roast Pork with Basil and Mushroom
    Stuffing, 111
Smoked Pork Loin Medallions with
    Maple Walnut Butter, 112

POTATOES
Gourmet Potato Pancakes, 77
Mashed Potatoes, 108
Potato Dill Biscuits, 146
Potato Parmesan Muffins, 149
Sausage, Potatoes and Leeks, 113
Sweetheart Potatoes, 77

PUDDINGS
Bread Pudding with Tennessee
    Whiskey Sauce, 166
Momma Case's Biscuit Puddin', 23

PUMPKIN
D'Liteful Pumpkin Pie, 182
Farm Pumpkin Bread, 144
Harvest Bisque, 50
Indian Sugar Pumpkins, 114
Pumpkin Bread Roll, 144
Pumpkin Cheesecake Bars, 170
Pumpkin Squares, 170

RASPBERRY
Fresh Fruit Salad, 56
Raspberry-Almond Coffee Cake, 154
Raspberry Coffee Cake, 153
Raspberry Pie, 182

RICE
Indian Sugar Pumpkins, 114
Lima Bean Risotto, 75
Mother and Child Chicken, 92
Rice Timbales, 123
Risotto with Artichokes and Shrimp, 78
Shrimp and Spanish Rice, 19
Three-Pepper Rice Salad, 67
Yakiniku Donburi [Fried Beef and
    Vegetables on Rice], 102

ROLLS
Refrigerator Rolls, 148
Rocky Mountain Icebox Rolls, 148

SALADS
Duck and Warm Brie Salad, 62
Panzanella, 63
Southwest Salad, 68
Three-Pepper Rice Salad, 67

SALADS, FRUIT
Berry Cool Summer Salad, 55
Fat-Free Fruit Salad, 55
Fresh Fruit Salad, 56
Fruit Blizzard, 56
Pan Salad, 14

SALADS, PASTA
Al's Shrimp and Crab Pasta Salad, 65
Pizza Pasta Salad Supreme, 64
Southwestern Pasta Salad, 66

Index

SALADS, VEGETABLE
Cucumber and Tomato Salad, 60
Gazpacho Salad, 60
Grilled Summer Salad, 61
Layered Corn Bread Salad, 59
Sweet and Savory Broccoli Salad, 57
Tangy Lemon Coleslaw, 58
Warm Broccoli Mushroom Salad, 57

SALSA
Meryll's Garden Salsa, 20
Papaya Salsa, 118
Pineapple and Green Tomato Salsa, 119

SAUSAGE
Beef and Sausage Shish Kabobs, 106
Eggs Fiesta, 16
Louisiana Gumbo, 49
Miss Penny's Sausage Stuffing, 81
Pasta Yaya, 135
Sauerkraut Casserole, 113
Sausage, Potatoes and Leeks, 113

SHELLFISH. *See also* Crab Meat;
Shrimp
Caribbean Seafood Stew, 51
Crawfish Cakes with Key Lime
Mustard Sauce, 126
Crawfish Gumbo, 48
Rasta Pasta, 128
Seafood Basil Pasta à la
Hummell, 127

SHRIMP
Al's Shrimp and Crab Pasta Salad, 65
Caribbean Seafood Stew, 51
Curried Shrimp and Chicken, 121
Louisiana Gumbo, 49
Pesto, Prawns, Prosciutto and
Pasta, 127
Pineapple Barbecue Shrimp, 122
Risotto with Artichokes and
Shrimp, 78
Shrimp and Spanish Rice, 19

Shrimp Chowder, 51
Shrimp Rémoulade with Vegetable
Rice Timbales, 123
Shrimp Scampi, 122
Shrimp Stroganoff, 20
Spaghetti Al Picchi Pacchio, 129

SIDE DISHES
Apple Stuffing, 81
Cranberry Pears, 84
Miss Penny's Sausage Stuffing, 81
Quick Corn Relish, 84
Spinach Grits, 78

SOUPS
Barb Wire's Real Texas-Style
Chili, 46
Black Bean Chili with Beer and
Chipotle Peppers, 45
Caesar's Symphony Soup, 53
Cannellini and Crab Meat Soup, 43
Caribbean Seafood Stew, 51
Chicken and White Bean Stew with
Cilantro and Basil, 47
Chilled Corn Chowder, 47
Christmas Chili, 12
Corky's Fifteen-Bean Soup, 41
Cream of Carrot Soup, 44
Deep South Chicken Stew, 44
Fresh Strawberry Soup, 54
Harvest Bisque, 50
Nancy and George Jones' Favorite
Soup, 43
Pasta-Vegetable Soup, 12
Roasted Tomato and White Bean
Soup, 42
Shrimp Chowder, 51
Spicy Southwestern Chowder, 52
Stracciatella [Italian Egg Drop
Soup], 53
Sunset Grill Basic Chili, 45
Thirty-Minute Beef and Black Bean
Soup, 41
Vegetarian Chili, 13

SPREADS
Baked Brie with Apple Chutney, 36

STRAWBERRY
Berry Cool Summer Salad, 55
Fat-Free Fruit Salad, 55
Fresh Strawberry Soup, 54
Strawberries Romanoff, 164
Strawberry Flambé, 163
Strawberry Lasagna, 163

SWEET POTATOES
Sweet Potato Biscuits, 147
Sweet Potato Casserole, 16
Sweet Potato Soufflé, 80

TARTS
Fruit Tart, 180
South Seas Chocolate Tarts, 179

TRIFLES
English Trifle, 172
Fantastic Trifle, 172

TURKEY
Corky's Fifteen-Bean Soup, 41
Fettuccini "What's To Cook Tonight," 132
Mid-Eastern Skillet Dinner, 109
Turkey Tortilla Casserole, 99

VEGETABLES. *See also* Individual
Kinds; Salads, Vegetable
Asparagus Casserole, 15
Bean-Stuffed Cabbage Rolls, 72
Cabbage Casserole, 71
Fried Green Tomatoes Stuffed with
Herb Cheese, 83
Miss Daisy's Party Squash, 79
Risotto with Artichokes and Shrimp, 78
Spinach Grits, 78
Stuffed Yellow Squash, 79
Stuffed Zucchini, 83
Swiss Vegetable Medley, 80
Tofu Stir-Fry, 82

TASTE OF THE TOWN

474 James Robertson Parkway
Nashville, Tennessee 37219

Please send _____ copies of *Taste of the Town* @ $15.95 each _____

Plus postage and handling of $4.00 each _____

TN residents add sales tax $1.32 each _____

Total _____

Make checks payable to: **Talk of the Town**

Name_____

Address _____

City_____ State _____ Zip Code_____

Telephone Number _____

TASTE OF THE TOWN

474 James Robertson Parkway
Nashville, Tennessee 37219

Please send _____ copies of *Taste of the Town* @ $15.95 each _____

Plus postage and handling of $4.00 each _____

TN residents add sales tax $1.32 each _____

Total _____

Make checks payable to: **Talk of the Town**

Name_____

Address _____

City_____ State _____ Zip Code_____

Telephone Number _____

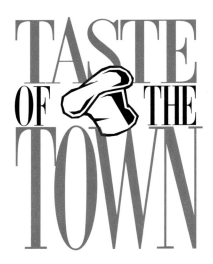